Apples and Avalanches

An Exploration of Caring for the Severely Mentally Ill

Heather Scherf, MS, LPC

BALBOA.PRESS
A DIVISION OF HAY HOUSE

Balboa Press books may be ordered through booksellers or by contacting:

Balboa Press
A Division of Hay House
1663 Liberty Drive
Bloomington, IN 47403
www.balboapress.com
844-682-1282

Print information available on the last page.

ISBN: 979-8-7652-3290-3 (sc)
ISBN: 979-8-7652-3291-0 (e)

Balboa Press rev. date: 08/15/2022

Dedication

This book is dedicated to all the souls who left this plane of existence too early due to the effects of severe mental health issues.

More specifically, this book is dedicated to my mother, Sandra Hubbard Allison.

In loving memory of a tenacious, kind, and loving mother, friend, spouse, and family member who just happens to be up in heaven right now dancing in stilettos.

Although you left, your presence is still felt in the ones who loved you. You imprinted the following ten lessons on us, and we carry them within our hearts.

1. Permanence, perseverance, and persistence in spite of all obstacles, discouragements, and impossibilities—in all things, these distinguish the strong souls from the weak.

2. The secret to happiness, you see, is not found in seeking more but in developing the capacity to enjoy less.
3. One of the greatest regrets in life is being what others would want you to be rather than being yourself. So be yourself.
4. Often I have asked myself, What would it be like if I no longer had any desire to judge another? Or to be controlled by the judgments of others? I would walk the Earth as a very light person indeed.
5. There is a nobility in compassion, a beauty in empathy, a grace in forgiveness.
6. Be fearless in the pursuit of what sets your soul on fire.
7. Kindness is being someone who makes everyone feel like a somebody.
8. A gracious heart, a gentle spirit.
9. Circumstances don't make a person; they reveal a person.
10. Open your heart and invite God into every circumstance because, when God enters the scene, miracles happen.

Darlin', only the good die young.

"You see, people never leave you, darling."

We all are just kindred souls, particles of one another,
lessons of one another moving across the fabric of time
and space—each person giving us more to enhance
our souls, which in turn we then carry to the next.
I carry your heart; I carry it in my heart.
Then I carry it to the next heart.

Contents

Introduction

Apples and Avalanches: An Exploration of Caring for the Severely Mentally Ill provides a personal perception of how we go through life with mental health issues. It is a story of a woman who suffered from schizophrenia and cancer for several years and of her daughter's perception of things from a caregiver's position. Watching an avalanche fall slowly is a metaphor for witnessing a loved one with mental health problems slowly deteriorate and the complications associated with it. And the apple doesn't fall far from the tree, referring to the children, spouses, and other loved ones who feel their own mental health deteriorating.

In the mental health world, we are always anticipating what will happen next in the process. *Anticipation grief* refers to a feeling of grief occurring before an impending loss. When we love someone with a mental illness, we suffer many forms of loss as symptoms increase in intensity over time—most noticeably, the loss of parts of the person we love. Furthermore, this can occur for weeks, months, years, or decades depending on the diagnosis.

I am writing from my personal experience, as well as my work as a licensed professional counselor in the state of Pennsylvania. I am a practicing clinician at a private practice in Western Pennsylvania. I currently see clients of every age and stage of development, from age three and up. I work with clients experiencing life-adjustment issues, grief and loss, and marriage or relationship issues and other individuals and families across varying diagnoses and needs. And across all those stages of development a few things remain the same: we all experience grief and loss, we all know someone who has a mental health diagnosis, and we are all just trying to heal from something.

I hope you find this book relatable and useful and that it provides some type of hope for you at the time you need it. This book is for families and caregivers of those with mental health issues. In it, I tell a story about an incredible woman in a way that is eclectic in nature, and you, the reader, can take what resonates and leave what does not.

This book is sectioned into three major parts. In each chapter are journal questions, or moments of reflection, for you to explore your thoughts and feelings on the subject matter. Some chapters have interactive activities throughout the content.

The first section, Avalanches, provides a narrative of my personal story with watching my mother suffer from mental illness. This section reflects upon barriers to mental health laws and the levels of care for individuals with mental illness.

The second section, Apples, focuses more specifically on you, the caregiver. This section presents several interactive tools to help you through caregiving and any correlating mental health symptoms you may face in the journey.

The third section, Healing Tools for the Future, explores how we can modify future care for those with severe mental illness and their family members for more well-rounded treatment.

In this book, readers will explore and learn several tools and concepts to help on the caregiving journey. You will learn how to set boundaries with loved ones with mental illness, how to reframe symptoms of mental illness so you can see the person for who they truly are and have a deeper understanding, choose from a "scrapbook" of tools and interventions to help you with your own mental health in the process of caregiving for a loved one, and gain tools to help you and your loved ones regulate your nervous systems as individuals and together during various stages of the journey.

The tools provided are eclectic in nature and pulled from many theories of psychology. Yet, the theories are specifically applied to loved ones of those with Mental illness so that the book can provide an interactive nature for you. There is also an optional survey for readers based on your experience in the caregiving journey in mental health at the end of the book. It gives you an opportunity to provide pieces of your story to share with others in an anonymous format.

My intention is that, while reading this book, you will feel seen, valued, and heard. I hope that this book serves as a guide for you to tell your own narrative story for healing and comfort. I want to share with you things I wish I had known or done differently in my journey to help you avoid more crises than are necessary.

Unconditional Love

What drove us here in the first place? How did we arrive at reading a self-help book on caring for the mentally ill? Well, the answer is simple—love. And not just love, but the unconditional kind of love. Love drove you here, not hatred. You are here because you are struggling with how to continue loving your loved one while simultaneously loving yourself.

We all are just love. It is what we are made of underneath all of whom or what we think we are. You, I, they, them—everything we touch is made of love. From the bench you sit on to drink your morning coffee, the clothes you wear to work, the house you live in, all of that is love as it was made from someone's creativity, and creation itself is love. And love is a state of being.

What is unconditional love? By definition, it is "affection without any limitations, or love without conditions" (Wikipedia 2022). In Christianity, it is considered part of the four types of love: affection, friendship, eros, and charity.

Christianity says unconditional love is "affection without any limitations," and Buddhism says unconditional love is "a general concern for another person's well-being" (Yogapedia 2022). Carl Rogers, a humanistic psychologist, says unconditional love and unconditional positive regard are the "basic acceptance and support of a person regardless of what the person says or does" (Cherry 2022). And Buddhism's word for "love" is *mettā*, meaning "friendly," "amiable," "benevolent," "affectionate," "kind," and "good-willed"(Yogapedia, 2022). It is also a form of love, amity, and sympathy.

For loving a family member with mental illness, I view unconditional love as meaning, "I love your soul unconditionally, the person you are underneath and through all those symptoms. I don't want to leave the house right now and pick you up to help you because of your hallucinations or delusions, but I am going to go anyway."

What is unconditional love to you?

To the mom of a child with autism, what are the ways you show your child unconditional love on a daily basis?

To the spouse of a person with mental illness, what are the ways you show unconditional love to your spouse?

To the parent of an adult child with addictions, what about you?

To anyone out there loving someone with any mental health or behavioral issues, how are you showing up every day with love?

The truth of the matter is that we all love our loved ones with mental health issues. *Yet we don't always like them.* And that is the natural part of the human experience. That is okay. It's normal. Yet we all show up in ways we feel we need to at the frequency and rate we feel we should, given the time and resources we know or have.

And I pose a question for you, readers: Are boundaries needed in matters of love? The traditional answer is a *yes*, right? I have found in my work as a therapist that people are always looking for a book about boundaries to establish with a family member or loved one with a mental health issue. The book options are apparently sparse.

This is maybe a better way to say it: yes, boundaries are needed for your own self-care in everything you do in life. But boundaries are not necessarily feasible in moments where unconditional love supersedes. We need boundaries to keep ourselves sane.

There is a need for a book to speak on this topic, *to speak directly to the pain that loved ones of people who have a mental health diagnosis endure.* Yet what if I told you the reality is that the book you may be seeking isn't about boundaries but about *how in the actual hell* you can get through this chaos; how you get through the pain while still holding space for the person you love; how you take care of this person and not feel guilty for the things you cannot emotionally, physically, or spiritually take on; and how you protect your energy and your heart yet still show unconditional love to the loved one in your care?

It's all just one big ball of incongruity. It is a fight between wanting to maintain your own sanity and caring for the other person. We wrestle with the shame and doubt that come with those needs existing simultaneously. That is the boundary we all seek in these matters of the heart. It's a push-pull mess of guilt.

Love is just energy. "As you continue to send out love, the energy returns to you in a generating spiral. As love accumulates, it keeps your system in balance and harmony. Love is the tool, and more love is the end product" (Paddision 1998).

When I think of people looking for a book on boundaries specific to mental health caregiving, I envision people looking for ten concrete ways to say no and what to do. We are all searching for this black-and-white answer to help be a guiding light in making choices surrounding our loved ones. But love is our guiding light. It's what even drives us to want this kind of help. Love is a vibration.

Boundaries have to change across time and space. There are no set rules by which to govern yourself while caretaking for a person with mental illness. The individual and intricate needs change daily. Boundaries should be tailored to the day ahead, moment to moment. You have to ask yourself daily, *What is my energy for this today? What is my ability to give specifically today?* It fluctuates depending on the symptoms present and how much you want to protect your energy. And later in this book, I will talk about compassion-led boundary setting.

I did not view things this way during my caretaking years with my mother, who suffered with schizophrenia. And I do not in any way, shape, or form want to paint myself as a saint in this story. I will set my intention of this book now: I am taking you on a journey through some of the darker parts of my story—a moment of true vulnerability in order to help you feel seen, valued, heard, and unalone. I made many errors in my life while caretaking for my mother. I had to face demons at various points, and I made choices that I regret.

This story comes from having a parent with a diagnosis of schizophrenia and, therefore, offers a very specific lens. However, my intent is to speak to anyone who has loved anyone with any mental health issues or diagnoses.

Reading this book may at moments make you feel triggered due to any trauma you have experienced in your life or your caretaking experience. If that happens, allow yourself a break from it. I hope this book provides some healing for you.

This book is meant to be "a conversation between friends." In the movie *The Shack*, in the scene called "A Garden of You," the Holy Spirit is talking to the main character, Mack, a grieving father. The garden is demonstrating the complexity of human emotions, as well as the necessity of feeling both pain and happiness (Hazeldine 2017).

Upon seeing a poisonous plant, Mack asks, "What's it doing here if it's poisonous?" which leads to a discussion of good versus evil. The Holy Spirit responds, "Your question presumes that poison is bad, that such creations have no purpose. Many of these so-called bad plants, like this one, contain incredible properties for healing or are necessary for some of the most magnificent sonders when combined with something else. Humans have a great capacity for declaring good or evil without knowing.... This garden is your soul. This mess is you! Together, you and I we have been working with a purpose in your heart. And it is wild and beautiful and perfectly in process."

The Holy Spirit talked about how humans weren't meant to judge things as good or evil and have wars. They were only meant to ever have "conversations between friends." So I relate this to my intentions for this book. I am not here to decide or judge what is good or evil. I am here to invite conversations among friends.

Adversity

If you are reading this book, you have faced adversity. It's what led you here.

You have been a silent, humble rock star for a very long time.

You have been facing situations and events that other people know nothing about.

You have fought battles in your heart and soul that no one knows about.

You have picked yourself up off the floor crying more times than anyone knows.

You have had to keep yourself balanced while simultaneously balancing the needs of others.

Let me introduce you to my mother, Sandy Hubbard Allison, and her adversity and resiliency. I will tell you a quick ten ways I have seen her adversity so I can introduce you to her beautiful soul.

- When her car broke down, she still had to go grocery shopping. She didn't ask for help. Instead, she rolled her suitcase up a main highway road to the grocery store, loaded it up, and rolled it back home.
- She sat in courthouses fighting for things that her hallucinations and delusions told her that were happening. She sat for hours in court filing petitions on things she thought were reality.
- When she was diagnosed with cancer, she got every treatment possible for it. She would do research on her own and was a fighter.
- Some people would talk about her schizophrenia right in front of her, as if she weren't sitting right there. Medical professionals were rude to her, yet she continued to keep her head up.
- While in the behavioral health hospital at the start of the COVID-19 pandemic in March 2020, her

body full of cancer and her symptoms intense, she still demanded an attorney to assert her rights, wanting to get out and wanting justice.

- She would find a way with her last dollar to go to a local bakery and get cookies for everyone on holidays.
- She would find things to sell just to get money to go down to Pittsburgh for the day to get out of the house.
- She was sexually assaulted at age four and had to deal with those demons her entire life.
- She came from poverty and rose to getting her real-estate license. She worked through her psychosis and paranoia regarding her job, yet she kept showing up daily for it.
- At the end, her body was full of cancer, and up until the last week of her life, she was still trying to escape our home. I had put weights in front of the door so she could not escape. Yet she still muscled up every last bit of strength to move those weights out of the way to "get out of here" and "go live."

Some struggles I had along the way are below.

- Digging deep to find a way to compassionate caregiving or continuing even when I had zero compassion left in the moment
- Finding a way to deal with my anger and resentment toward the illness and, at times, toward her
- Trying to see her as a person, a soul, and not as her illness (seeing through the symptoms)

- Trying to work through resentment toward her for not meeting my emotional needs as a child and causing some inner childhood wounds
- Worrying that I would end up with mental health problems myself, due to the genetic background of mental health in my family
- Wrestling with not being able to have any logical, emotional, or meaningful dialogue with her because of her symptoms
- Longing for goodbyes when she was in her final days before passing
- Questioning God and spirituality on why she had to suffer two debilitating illnesses at once
- Victimizing myself, living in anxiety and fear
- Suffering from issues surrounding self-worth, shame, and guilt in the process of caregiving
- Wrestling with my attachment wounds and anxious attachment style

But through this storytelling, I want readers to see how it played out for her and me. *Take what resonates in the story, and leave what doesn't. If something doesn't fit, don't try to make it fit.* Take what you need, and leave what you don't.

I will end this section with a final thought on love. Love is shown by people, in the best way they know how, at the time they are loving you. They might not know how to love you the way you need or want, so they use the resources they have to love the best they can at that specific time. And ironically, this is true for adversity as well. We do the best we can do at the time with the resources we have to face our struggles and situations.

Moment of Reflection

1. What have you had to sacrifice while caring for a person with mental health issues?
2. What worst parts of you have come out during that process?
3. What have you had to heal within yourself in order to keep going?
4. What are you still in process of healing as part of your journey with this?
5. What hardships have you faced in caregiving?
6. What are the things that have made you feel angry, hurt, fearful, or resentful in this process?
7. What is the adversity your loved one had to face during their journey with mental health?
8. How have you supported yourself thus far in your caregiving experience?

Important Definitions and Statistics

Before moving into chapter 1, a few definitions and general statistics are needed to ensure we are all on the same page.

The National Institute of Mental Health provides the following definitions:

> Any Mental Illness is (AMI) is defined as a mental, behavioral, or emotional disorder. AMI can vary in impact, ranging from no impairment to mild, moderate, and even severe impairment.

Severe/Serious Mental Illness is (SMI) is defined as a mental, behavioral, or emotional disorder resulting in serious functional impairment, which substantially interferes with or limits one or more major life activities. The burden of mental illnesses is particularly concentrated among those who experience disability due to SMI. ("Mental Health" 2022)

The National Alliance of Mental Illness provides the following data:

The prevalence of AMI in 2020 was 1 in 5 adults each year, or 52.9 million adults in the US.

Youth ages 6-17 experience mental illness at a rate of 1 out of 6 children, or 7.7 million people.

The prevalence of SMI in 2020 was 1 in 20 adults each year, or 14.2 million people in the US.

Schizophrenia is a serious mental illness that affects how a person thinks, feels, and behaves. People with schizophrenia may seem like they have lost touch with reality, which causes significant distress for the individual, their family members, and friends.… 1 in 100 adults live with schizophrenia, or 2.4 million Americans (in 2020). ("Mental Health by the Numbers" 2022)

Psychosis

The National Institute of Mental Health provides this regarding psychosis:

> The word psychosis is used to describe conditions that affect the mind, where there has been some loss of contact with reality. When someone becomes ill in this way it is called a psychotic episode. During a period of psychosis, a person's thoughts and perceptions are disturbed and the individual may have difficulty understanding what is real and what is not.

Symptoms of psychosis include delusions (false beliefs) and hallucinations (seeing or hearing things that others do not see or hear). Other symptoms include incoherent or nonsense speech, and behavior that is inappropriate for the situation. A person in a psychotic episode may also experience depression, anxiety, sleep problems, social withdrawal, lack of motivation, and difficulty functioning overall. ("Mental Health" 2022)

The symptoms of schizophrenia generally fall into the following three categories:

Psychotic symptoms include altered perceptions (e.g., changes in vision, hearing, smell, touch, and taste), abnormal thinking, and odd behaviors. People with psychotic symptoms may lose a shared sense of reality and experience themselves and the world in a distorted way. Specifically, individuals typically experience:

- Hallucinations, such as hearing voices or seeing things that aren't there
- Delusions, which are firmly held beliefs not supported by objective facts (e.g., paranoia—irrational fears that others are "out to get you" or believing that the television, radio, or internet is broadcasting special messages that require some response)
- Thought disorder, which includes unusual thinking or disorganized speech

Negative symptoms include loss of motivation, disinterest or lack of enjoyment in daily activities, social withdrawal, difficulty showing emotions, and difficulty functioning normally. Specifically, individuals typically have:

- Reduced motivation and difficulty planning, beginning, and sustaining activities
- Diminished feelings of pleasure in everyday life
- "Flat affect," or reduced expression of emotions via facial expression or voice tone
- Reduced speaking

Cognitive symptoms include problems in attention, concentration, and memory. For some individuals, the cognitive symptoms of schizophrenia are subtle, but for others, they are more prominent and interfere with activities like following conversations, learning new things, or remembering appointments. Specifically, individuals typically experience:

- Difficulty processing information to make decisions
- Problems using information immediately after learning it
- Trouble focusing or paying attention

Some common misconceptions exist about schizophrenia and other disorders that have psychosis as part of their symptoms. People with severe mental health issues are not dangerous. It's not a form of mental retardation, dementia, delirium, or intoxication, nor a personality disorder. People can and do recover from Schizophrenia. It's also not contagious ("What Schizophrenia Is Not" 2022).

People living with schizophrenia can still make their own decisions about treatment and their lives. They can still work and live normal lives. They do not need to be institutionalized. They can have conversations with you and hear you when you speak, even if they are experiencing psychotic symptoms at that time. Some individuals with psychosis can recognize their symptoms and discern what is reality depending on where they are in their treatment and journey.

While this book does not aim to define everything about mental health, it is important to know some basic information about psychosis and schizophrenia before reading on.

Trauma

Trauma is an emotional response to a terrible event like an accident, rape, or a natural disaster. Immediately after the event, shock and denial are typical. Longer-term reactions include unpredictable emotions, flashbacks, strained relationships, and even physical symptoms like headaches or nausea (APA 2022).

There are three types of trauma: acute, chronic, and complex. Acute trauma results from a single event, such as witnessing a natural disaster, that causes symptoms. Chronic trauma comes from repeated or prolonged exposure to situations such as domestic violence or abuse, and complex trauma is a result of exposure to varied and multiple types of traumatic events, often of an invasive and interpersonal nature.

It is important to note that two people can witness the exact same event or natural disaster but view it differently and have different psychological, emotional, and physical responses to it. Trauma is in the eye of the beholder. What one person may view as traumatic, the next might not.

When it comes to potential trauma related to having a loved one with a mental illness, it can get complex in nature and vary greatly depending on individual experiences. Not everyone who has taken care of a loved one with mental illness views the experience as traumatic. Yet many people do. It is a form of relational trauma.

Before reading on, I think it is important to take inventory of your own sense of trauma. As reading this book may bring up difficult feelings for you, memories, or other triggers, it is important to allow yourself breaks from reading if you feel yourself becoming dysregulated emotionally or feel somatic symptoms or discomfort. And seek a professional therapist to support you and talk over these feelings.

Now that we are on the same page in terms of what mental illness is and what psychosis is, we can move on to working through how they affect us. I will first tell Mom's story while trying to present relatable points to you of what it's like to love and care for someone whose mental health is deteriorating rapidly. The purpose is not to create a memoir but rather for you to relate to parts of the story.

Conclusion

I mentioned the statistics of individuals suffering from mental illness in our country. In terms of caregivers, there are roughly 8.4 million of us who provide care to an adult with a severe mental or emotional health issue. On average, caregivers spend thirty-two hours per week providing unpaid care to their loved ones. These are just the statistics on the individuals with more severe mental health problems. How much do you spend per week caretaking for your loved one with a mental health issue?

I issue a call to action for yourself and our loved ones. My hope is that mental health law, policies and procedures, and access-to-care issues change for the sake of those suffering. I also hope that levels of care or treatment can shift into more time-oriented circumstances that are unique to each individual needing help and that those levels of care start to offer more holistic multidisciplinary options of treatment. I hope and pray that you share your story with anyone who can make changes to our system.

PART ONE

Avalanches

1

Mom's Story

It's important that I tell my mother's story to illustrate the trauma and chaos of mental illness. This chapter aims to illustrate a few key points: how the avalanche fell slowly across several decades of her life, how her symptoms manifested in different ways across time, and the level of difficulty in getting a loved one with mental illness appropriate care. A very important point is the level of intelligence and resourcefulness my mother had to possess to be able to avoid treatment for decades. I hope that, while you are reading this chapter, you find relatable points within your own story to reflect upon.

My mom's name is Sandra Hubbard Allison, and she was born in 1955. She grew up in a small town called Wilkinsburg near Pittsburgh, Pennsylvania, as part of a low-income family. She was a majorette and active in other clubs throughout her schooling. She was an avid

Pittsburgh sports enthusiast; she loved her Steelers, Penguins, and Pirates!

She loved putting on a nice pair of shoes and going to concerts to dance with her friends. She also loved traveling and taking adventures of any kind—she lived life to the fullest. She especially loved cooking and baking for her loved ones.

She worked at Mine Safety Appliances in Murrysville, PA, for many years. From there she went to college to obtain her associate's degree in advertising and then her real estate license. She later worked in advertising for newspapers in the Philadelphia and Pittsburgh areas and then as a Realtor in the Monroeville area.

She was married three times, once to her first love for a short period of time. Second was my father, Keith, and third was Ron, the true love of her life. She got together with Ron when I was about three, and they were together from 1985 to 2012, so twenty-seven years. Unfortunately, the illness she had caused difficulties in the marriage and ultimately led to its end. I am her only child.

My mother had a burning passion for life. She is most known for her many years of dancing at the infamous Holiday Inn in Pittsburgh. She wore the best and most flashy outfits, along with her stilettoes, and would light up a room. Her attitude and spirit were infectious to others.

She also, unfortunately, had a diagnosis of a debilitating mental illness, paranoid schizophrenia.

I am sad that I didn't ask her more questions about her upbringing and that certain conversations could not be held due to her illness. I will only be writing what I know about in her history.

She was sexually abused at age four. Our family lineage includes loved ones who have passed away but who also suffered from mental illness and trauma (schizophrenia, depression, abuse). And I come from and am woven from that same cloth. I wish there were more details like this and that our lineage could have been reviewed before my mother's passing. But the point is that my mother faced her own inner demons as a result of a long history of mental health issues.

How we look at and define mental health will be reviewed later in this book. Yet, for now, I posit these questions of reflection for you: What is the lineage of mental health that runs in your family of origin? What is the lineage of mental health in your spouse's family of origin? Just keep this in mind, as throughout the book we will be revisiting these pasts and ideas.

My mom was diagnosed in 1999 with paranoid schizophrenia after she hospitalized herself. She was forty-four years old at the time of her first diagnosis. This is *extremely rare* with schizophrenia, as typically people present symptoms much earlier in life (adolescent to young adulthood years).

My stepfather was married to her at the time, and I was living with my father and stepmother in Pennsylvania.

They were living in Kentucky. My stepfather told me that the first time she displayed symptoms of psychosis was after she used cocaine in a hotel room. She began displaying paranoia about police and other people coming to the hotel room to arrest her and other similar things.

My mother also had a history of alcoholism and addictions. In hindsight, I know they were just to numb the pain she felt from her early childhood trauma. I can remember her falling ill from alcoholism at Steeler games when I was younger. I remember her driving us home from a bowling alley when I was in second grade, and she was drunk at the wheel. While she lived life to the fullest, alcohol was her demon. She occasionally used cocaine and marijuana. Yet I was never aware of this until much later in life.

After the hospitalization in Kentucky, she and Ron moved to Philadelphia for different job opportunities. She was still suffering from her illness and drinking. She had eight car accidents and two driving under intoxication charges in a short length of time. She was even on house arrest for sixty days at one point as a result.

In 2001, she was hospitalized with her first 302 (involuntary placement) by her husband, Ron. She had aggressed toward him, stabbed him in the head with keys, and hit him.

My mother's hallucinations and delusions unfortunately surrounded Ron. Her symptoms would tell her that Ron was stealing her real estate customers, cheating or having affairs, and stealing money and settlements from her.

Earlier on in the first years, she had approximately three voices in her mind.

Fast-forward nine years to 2010, when she had her second 302 hospitalization. This time, she had tried to kill my stepfather. She put glass from a broken picture frame in his bed and made verbal threats to "blow his head off and cut off his balls." She also reportedly poisoned his breakfast.

Now, I want to pause in this story for a moment and highlight a very important point to ensure understanding. My mother and people with mental illness are not dangerous. The reason she aggressed toward my stepfather was that the hallucinations would tell her that he was hurting her in various ways. So in her mind, it was self-perseveration and self-protection. Every person's journey with severe mental health problems is different. You have to understand that my mother was not a violent person by nature. And the last thing I want to do in this book is paint mental illness more in the darkness than it already is.

It is extremely noteworthy that from 2001 to 2010 was a *nine*-year span of time in which she did not get treatment, had no medications, and lived and functioned with her illness. My stepfather had grown tired of the mental health system at this time. He did not see any value in continuing to try and hospitalize her, expecting different results. And this is a failure of our mental health system that I will speak about later. But that was nine years of difficulties that they both faced and suffered in silence. I do and will forever have empathy for my stepfather for fighting that battle alone. He fought battles that I know nothing about. He lived in fear with his doors locked because her symptoms were manifesting toward him. He truly has a story of his own that needs to be told and heard and seen by others.

I did not find out about my mother's illness until I was in graduate school for counseling. It was in 2007, and I was roughly twenty-five years old. Because I had lived with my father and stepmother from age twelve on and she and Ron lived out of state, I knew nothing for all of those years. I was oblivious. After a few conversations with my mother that sounded off, as she was talking about Ron stealing from her and making other strange statements, Ron finally opened up to me and told me some of the history.

At that moment, I remember feeling so fearful of her. Even being in a counseling master's program, learning how to be a counselor in mental health, I still was cloaked with complete fear—fear of not understanding schizophrenia, fear of what others would think, fear of her symptoms, fear she would wrap me up in her hallucinations, and many others. It took me years, and ultimately until her passing, to truly grasp and understand what was happening.

Fast-forward to 2012 and 2013, when Ron and my mother separated and divorced. The seven years from roughly 2013 through the date of her passing, December 17, 2020, are the ones about which I want to have a heart-to-heart with you. These are the "Mom and I" years. The avalanche fell slowly as I watched her decline, and the apple (me) fell and remained close to the tree.

Some writers say the best writing isn't chronological. Yet I need to tell this story in order of what occurred so you can see the avalanche I refer to and the nature of psychosis, as it is hard to understand to begin with.

Before this roughly eight-year time frame, the avalanche had already started falling slowly. Then, during the last four years of her life, from 2016 to 2020, it crashed at the bottom of the mountain. For the first few years, she was able to sustain a somewhat routine life. She had an apartment on her own, worked in real estate, and kept herself overall safe. She was very symptomatic with her psychosis yet still able to function in day to day. She would run out of money occasionally, her car would break down, or she would need help doing her laundry, but otherwise she was good.

During this time period, she began filing petitions at court against the voices she heard. The number of voices she heard increased as years went by. By the time she was close to passing, I think there were about twenty.

In April of 2017, she was diagnosed with stage 4 cancer, specifically a neuro-endocrine tumor and orbital mass. The cancer started in her left eye, liver, and pancreas before spreading to her shoulder, back, and other parts of her body. The cancer was an extremely rare type related to the left eye.

From that moment on, the symptoms of her two very debilitating diseases intertwined and overlapped. She grew to have delusions and hallucinations surrounding her cancer, her doctors, and her treatment team.

For example, my mother experienced schizophrenia in the following way. She had hallucinations and delusions regarding the government, her ex-husband, and other random people she would encounter over time. She believed that these individuals and entities had worked together to hurt her, traumatize her, abuse her, steal from her, manipulate her, and torture her. Over the years the individuals within her mind changed slightly or shifted onto different people.

Pause for a moment. Can you imagine living like this? Honestly believing that all these people want to hurt you and cause you pain in some way? I couldn't. Living in fear constantly, daily, hourly, and minute by minute?

Her first hallucinations and delusions were about her ex-husband and other entities. Ron and several others were her voices for many years. My mother believed that they were working together to steal money and real-estate leads from her and that they were hoarding multi-million-dollar settlements from her.

Her voices started out with this theme. She would argue with her voices out loud when no one was around and make off-putting, random comments in the presence of others. When this would happen around family members or friends, both my stepfather and I would give her a light nudge to the arm to redirect her thinking to something else. This was an effective intervention to hide her issues from others for a good year or two, until it wasn't. But it sure wasn't an effective intervention for her. It was clearly meant to hide our own shame and embarrassment about the illness. What we experienced will be addressed later.

To illustrate a typical dialogue in my mother's mind on a daily, sometimes hourly, sometimes minute-to-minute basis, see below.

This first example is a minor illustration.

Mom: "Stop it! Just stop it! I'm going to report you!"

Anonymous voice: *No, you won't. It's our money, and you will not get any of it.*

Ron's voice: *Ha ha, she thinks she's going to get that money, and she's not.*

The second example is from 2019, eighteen years later, with unmedicated and untreated symptoms as well as cancer:

Anonymous voice: *Ha ha, we got away with it. We have her money.*

Ron's voice: *Yeah, and we also put that device in her body to make her stool hurt.*

Judge's voice: *You guys have to give me part of the money and I won't vote that she gets any of it.*

Landlord's voice: *You owe six months' rent!*

Government official's voice: *We can put another device in her this weekend to get her sick again.*

Police officer's voice: *Yeah, that sounds like a good plan.*

Mom: "I am going to sue all of you, and you are all going to hell!"

While this isn't the exact dialogue, it's just a small picture of what she listened to every single minute of her waking hours. She constantly heard six or more voices arguing with one another, in her mind, about hurting her in some way.

I have probably witnessed over a thousand of these conversations and arguments over the past several years. She eventually got to the point that she was unable to cognitively function and have a conversation about anything without being interrupted. She would also argue verbally aloud as if the person were standing right beside her. She would at times believe I was actively participating in those conversations with her.

During her last year of life, she was at my home, and we were sitting on the deck on a summer day. I was talking to her about my divorce, as she asked me about my life. When I was answering her question about something, she stood up and screamed in a loud, desperate, pleading voice, "Please stop it! I'm trying to talk to my daughter!" At that moment, I sat in silence, and my heart shattered into a million pieces thinking about how much she longed to be able to be there for me during my time of need but couldn't. She just couldn't. And it was no fault of her own. This will forever be a broken part of my heart, knowing that she wanted to do more but could not.

On the deck that day, she proceeded to have an approximately twenty-minute argument with the voices about the rent and money and torture they were all doing to her. I tried to redirect, but it was pointless. It had to run its course. So I sat there, observed, and internally screamed with my anxiety spiking and feeling helpless. I needed to walk away to give my mind a break from her mind.

Symptoms of both her illnesses continued to play against each other.

On a Sunday morning, I woke up and looked at my cell phone to see a few missed calls from my mother. One message stated, "Heather I am at the hospital, and I need you to come get me." The calls came in at about three o'clock that morning, but I woke up and saw them at about six. The messages did not specify what hospital or why she was there. She spoke in frantic tones. I called her a few times but got no answer. So I drove to her apartment. For that ten-minute drive, I was in a panic yet also in a state of being used to the chaos.

My intrusive thoughts went from *She's dead* to *She might have walked home from hospital and gotten kidnapped; I have no idea if she's at her apartment, at the hospital, or what hospital if at a hospital; I have no idea if this is cancer related or mental health related;* and *What if she got home and committed suicide?* There are probably a few more that I am not thinking of, but you get the point.

I got to the apartment and knocked on the door and windows, at first hearing no response. After a few tries, I heard her yell as if she thought I was one of her hallucinations or delusions, but she came to the door. I sat down with her. She looked awful—tired, disheveled, unclean. She explained what had happened.

"I called an ambulance last night because they put a device in my back yesterday and my poop got stuck. So the hospital gave me a stool softener and did a CT scan and the device isn't there anymore. The cop was supposed to take me home, but he left. So another person at the hospital was nice enough to give me a ride home."

My own inner dialogue went, *Breathe, Heather. Breathe before you respond. Think.* Then, getting angry, I thought, *What the fudge—they let her leave? She went into that hospital saying there was a device put in her back, she was potentially having a bowel issue related to her cancer, and the medical team just let her walk out of the hospital? I am listed as her emergency contact in all her medical records. Not one person stopped to think to look for that or was kind enough to look for that as to not let a mentally ill and cancerous patient leave the hospital room without a ride home? And not one person there thought to call her emergency contact when she was in crisis? And not one person thought it was medically necessary for her to stay the night? What is wrong with our system?*

My inner compassionate thought was, *Holy hell, Mom.* My inner sad thought was, *I have no idea what to do to help you right now.* And my inner realist thoughts were, *If the system cannot help, I can't either. So I will make sure she is okay for today and has her basic needs met for another day.*

It was a hundred-degree day, and she didn't have air conditioning in her apartment. So on top of her feeling like shit, it felt like 115 degrees in there. Off to Walmart I went to get her an air conditioner. Sometimes, that's all you can do—provide comfort in these times of crisis.

This was my mom's life day in and day out. Not a day went by that she experienced peace and calmness.

She was not "sick enough" to get forced treatment at that time. She wasn't threatening to hurt herself or anyone else. She was still meeting her own basic needs well enough (showering, taking cancer medications, proper hygiene). She was even still working in real estate. Thus, she was not sick enough to even be placed into a personal-care home. This was about two years prior to her passing.

The White House and "The Fixers"

As time progressed and cancer continued to spread throughout her body, a big shift occurred in her symptoms of psychosis. The themes of her hallucinations and delusions became much more embedded around her cancer.

"The fixers from the White House" is what she called the team of people who would come to visit her to help heal her cancer and bodily pain. She would sit upright in a specific chair and almost look like she was meditating. She would say, "The fixers are going to do my daily treatment." The fixers were the good guys. And as I am writing this out, I am realizing how much emotional comfort that brought her.

The more spiritual I become, the more I believe that the fixers were her guardian angels trying to relieve some of her mental and emotional anguish, even if only for a short time. Was it a placebo effect or truly her guardian angels at work? Either way, it was temporary relief for her.

As things progressed, her symptoms manifested in other ways. For example, as her belly got bigger from the cancer, she concluded that her voices had implanted a fetus and that she was pregnant. Her voices would tell her to eat only certain foods for the cancer, such as carrots out of a can.

The fridge in her apartment was broken at this time, but she did not call to get a new fridge because her voices kept telling her that one would be delivered. She waited weeks for this fridge that never came. In the interim, she placed a cooler outside with limited food in it, which worked since it was wintertime.

Similarly, her apartment was infested with roaches, and she kept hallucinating that pest control services were scheduled to come to the apartment. Thus, she did not actually follow through with calling a company to get help, and she would not accept help from me. These are just a few examples of how things declined quickly.

Moment of Total Impact: She Went Missing

Now, fast-forward to the year 2020. At this point, I had accessed every social-service agency in the area. The county's area agency on aging had been involved at one point, yet my mother did not want their assistance. She didn't want any type of service, help, or counseling. I couldn't yet do anything legal to obtain power of attorney or guardianship. Even though she wasn't eating, couldn't pay her bills, wasn't taking care of her body, didn't have a working fridge, and had a bug-infested apartment, that still wasn't bad enough to get legal and forced help.

I felt like she and I were screaming in the middle of a crowded room and no one even looked up (inspired by a *Titanic* quote). I know there is a slightly different context than Rose from *Titanic* here, yet I felt the same intensity of emotion that Rose did during these moments.

In March of 2020, my absolute worst fear became reality. I lost her. She was lost. It was the weekend of her birthday, March 1. A few days earlier, I had stopped over at her house to check on her and ask her what she wanted to do for her birthday. However, she wasn't there, and she wasn't answering her cell phone. The first time that week, I thought not much of it: *Oh, maybe she just took a bus to Pittsburgh for the day and isn't answering her phone.* So I left and waited to see if I'd hear from her. Two days later, I had still heard nothing back. I drove back down to her apartment, and the soup I had left at the door for her on the first trip was still in the same spot, untouched. Again, multiple attempts to reach her cell phone were unsuccessful.

I ultimately confided in my family and friends, and they agreed that it was time to file a missing person's report. I was totally ashamed and embarrassed that I had lost my mother. How could I have let this happen? Simultaneously, I wanted to rise from the ashes like Katniss Everdeen in the *Hunger Games*, yet instead of fighting a totalitarian government like she does in the movie, I wanted to fight the mental health system. I wanted to do this with every fiber of my being but was mainly worried about her and fearing the worst. My thoughts flooded with rage and anger toward every part of the mental-health system.

For the next two days—a Sunday and a Monday—I sat thinking she was dead in a ditch somewhere. It was a cold and snowy time in late winter. I had visions of her lying down by the river and other horrific details.

The police were actively looking for her. We had posted on social media that she was missing and asking people for help. And everyone helped. In that moment of chaos, angels everywhere were looking for her. My family and friends drove around locally, as did strangers who saw the social media posts and others. And I thought to myself, *Holy shit, there are so many good people out there.* My family, friends, and I were filled with so much gratitude for all the help from the community.

And later on that Monday afternoon, I received a call from the New Kensington Police Department saying that they had found her! Two local police departments worked together to find her. I immediately cried, of course, and collapsed to my knees. Miracles do happen every day. Thank God! Praise God! And I am forever grateful to those police departments.

She was found that afternoon walking on Rodi Road in Penn Hills. She had lost her cell phone prior to this, and when I saw her at the hospital on Monday evening, she told me, "I was talking to you through the device the whole time." She stated that she had left her keys inside her apartment, stayed at a hotel Friday night, and went to another hotel on Saturday night. I did not know what was true or where she had been; I was just glad she had been found safe.

Now, the prior Wednesday, she had been eating at a local restaurant and bar when her symptoms started acting up, and the bartender called an ambulance. She was experiencing severe derealization (detachment from reality and her surroundings) in the restaurant, and that kind bartender thought to call for help. She was then taken by ambulance to a hospital. The hospital fed her, and she stayed a night there. I was not called or notified by the hospital. No one reached out to her emergency contact. (Yet this is related to mental-health law. If someone isn't "bad enough," they are protected by the privacy laws, HIPAA.) The police are the ones who told me this while they were making calls to investigate tips we were getting on social media. From there she was discharged from the hospital, and she took a bus from one town to the next.

You see, my mom's reason for going in that direction to begin with was because she thought she was pregnant, at age sixty-four. Her voices told her that a fetus was implanted in her. She was going to a doctor in that area to "have the fetus removed." In hindsight, we know that her cancer had progressed and was affecting various parts of her body, which is what made her belly inflamed and feel as if she were pregnant. My heart was broken for her.

A lot about that situation could have been avoided. If our system were structured differently, then people with severe mental illness would be more supported in situations like this. Inclusion of family members when someone comes into a hospital in distress would be ideal—clearly. A few quick phone calls to an emergency contact could have avoided the involvement of the police department and community. How many times are situations like this going to occur in our country with the system we currently have?

Why? Why in our system do we allow these things to happen? I humbly add that I am a white, Caucasian, privileged woman in this country. Yet, regardless of race and socioeconomic status, the consequences of the mental health system continue to bring limited results to anyone suffering with severe mental illness. I only refer to my being white because I am educated and had a little bit of money to get legal help. Not everyone in these circumstances does. In fact, most do not.

Speaking of legal help, after the hospitalization occurred, I started the legal battle. This all occurred during the first couple weeks of COVID in March 2020. Mom was transferred to a behavioral health hospital that evening. Finally, she was "bad enough" to be 302'd. And I will add that, even at that hospital, the doctor assessed my mother and reported she wasn't bad enough to hospitalize. My loving stepmother was with me, and she and I had to beg the doctor to understand my mother's history. I am thankful to that doctor who ended up listening to us, hearing us, and having compassion toward us. This is just another example of how high-functioning people with schizophrenia can present themselves when they are being assessed as doing well and hide symptoms just enough to fool a doctor. Her going missing was the catalyst to her ultimate hospitalization. It took all those resources, police officers' time, and failing policy around medical and social services collective systems to get to this point.

I say it again, the avalanche has to fall before the clean-up services help in this country. We live in a reactive system, not a proactive system.

Process of Getting Legal Help

After her stay in the behavioral health hospital, I was able to obtain an attorney and begin fighting for legal guardianship of her. I finally could take that step forward to get legal decision-making rights over her care. It is not an easy process to obtain guardianship.

For someone to get legal guardianship over another, the person must be considered incapacitated. An "incapacitated person means an adult whose ability to receive and evaluate information effectively and communicate decisions in any way is impaired to such a significant extent that he is partially or totally unable to manage his financial resources or to meet essential requirements for his physical health and safety" (Commonwealth of Pennsylvania Code 231 Rule 14.6).

This must be proved by significant evidence and psychological evaluations. To do this, I supplied my attorney with a list of every single behavior and symptom I could think of, as well as a detailed list of Mom's mental health and legal history. The psychiatrist from the behavioral health hospital had to also get on board and fill out forms indicating he had evaluated her and determined she was incapacitated.

Fast-forward to the completion of all of that, when the next step is to sit in a courtroom facing the incapacitated parent on the other side. Well, for us, it was the beginning of COVID lockdown restrictions, so our court hearing was held via phone. Anyway, during that court process, I had to bear witness to the process of my attorney intentionally illuminating, provoking, and antagonizing her so that her symptoms would come out. After all, that's what I was paying her for. My attorney was amazing and did a great job. However, the entire process was shameful, embarrassing, and humiliating.

The lawyer said things such as, "Sandra, tell the court why you thought you were pregnant at age sixty-four," "Sandra, tell the court that your voices told you to stop eating," and, "Sandra, tell the judge about the fixers and the White House." This went on for quite some time. My mother would respond the way we needed her to, explaining her hallucinations and delusions as her reality.

I was winning in the court but not in my heart. I couldn't believe that this is what we as a society must do to the ones we love to get them help. We must completely humiliate them. My mother was smart. People with mental illness are smart. She knew that the court was trying to fight against her hallucinations and delusions, and can you imagine how small that made her feel? How insignificant? How hurt? Could you imagine feeling like no one understands you already, feeling isolated and alone because of your mental health, and then you walk into a courtroom and are further not seen or heard?

I understand that people have a right to defend themselves. I personally just don't understand why things must get so bad before someone can get help. Is this really needed in our system? Is there any other way to deem someone incapacitated without further shaming? Ugh. Maybe not. It just didn't seem needed.

Nonetheless, court ended, and I was given full legal guardianship over her and her estate, meaning I could make all necessary medical decisions for her and take care of any matters related to her apartment and belongings. I wonder how her heart felt knowing she had officially lost her independence. None of us like to do that to our parents or other loved ones. Yet, we must.

After obtaining legal rights over her needs, I moved her in to a personal care home. But we were in the thick of COVID, and personal care homes shut their doors to outside visitors for several months. While my mother was in there without visitors, her cancer was taking over her body. We all went long periods without seeing our loved ones. I finally saw her in August 2020, so almost five months from the date she was hospitalized. I didn't recognize her when I saw her. Her belly had grown from the cancer, but she was incredibly thin everywhere else.

For a couple of weeks, the home staff allowed me to spend additional time with her because of her prognosis. I visited her regularly from that point until, one day, I just couldn't emotionally handle leaving her there anymore and moved her home with me. I had the pleasure of caring for her through November and December until she passed away. I wouldn't change that time period for anything. I have no regrets about that.

You may wonder why I chose a personal care home at that time anyway. The simple answer is that I was burnt out. I did not have the emotional capacity at that time to take her home with me. I was working full time as a therapist. I could not handle dealing with others' mental health twenty-four-seven for all of my waking life after everything that had occurred over the past couple of years. So yes, this is a boundary I chose based on my need at that time.

While we were living together, there were moments when I was completely rude to her. There were also moments I got to care for her in different ways, such as curling her hair, scratching her back, and cooking her meals. At one point, all she would eat or drink was chocolate milk. And since chocolate is a diuretic, I would monitor how much she drank and set a cut-off time, or last call, for chocolate milk at 10:00 p.m. She would say, "You're cruel" in a soft, sweet voice.

And while this isn't a story about death and dying, I do want to share a few thoughts regarding being with someone who is dying. On December 17, 2020, my mother went to be with the Lord. It was a snowy morning, and now every year during the first snowfall of the year, I still remember her and feel a sense of peace. Only she and I were in the room when she passed. There is just something about watching the soul of someone you love leave their physical body and enter into heaven. You just know they are being relieved of all their pain and suffering and feeling nothing but light and love.

Now that I have shared Mom's timeline of events, I want to pause with you and allow some reflection time before we move on to the next chapter.

Moment of Reflection

1. Did you feel triggered by reading this story in any way?
2. What parts of Mom's story resonate within yourself or can you relate to?
3. What are your thoughts on the mental health system based on your experiences with it?
4. What avalanches have you had to watch?
5. If you are a social worker or therapist, what are your thoughts? What do you see?

2

Our Mental Health System

The last chapter demonstrates how the mental health system perpetuated my mother's issues and that we have a reactive system instead of a proactive, holistic system. We all know this. We are trying as a society to make changes to this. The evolution of levels within mental health care means changes take a long time.

As people who love others with mental health issues; as people experiencing mental health problems; and as providers, therapists, and social workers, we all see how our current system does not support overall wellness and holistic care. I have had many conversations with clients over the years regarding their own frustrations with many layers within the system that do not help, and for various reasons. This chapter aims to explore these very issues.

There are access-to-care issues relating to insurance coverage. There are staffing issues in the therapy and social-work fields, continuously, everywhere. There is a lack of consistency and availability of professionals due to scarcity. The programs that exist for individuals and families with severe mental health diagnoses are outpatient levels of care, dual diagnosis treatment centers, and intensive outpatient programs.

If we are truly honest with ourselves as people who are working in the helping professions, we all have that inner knowing that we are just doing the bare minimum at times to make sure our clients are stable *enough*—that they aren't wanting to kill themselves and are showering, eating, and getting through the week alive. I am not discounting the work we do; I am simply asking, Could we do better than what we are doing now as a collective whole? We all want to. It's the systems themselves that hold us back.

When clients with schizophrenia or any severe mental health diagnosis go into an outpatient clinic to get their medications (if they go), they typically have a fifteen-minute "med check" with the psychiatrist. The nurse takes their vital signs. The clients go in to quickly update the doctor on how they are feeling. They get their prescriptions and leave. They may or may not get their individual therapy for the week or month, depending on the specific program's rules and procedures. State laws and other factors across our country play into this.

The therapy appointments that do occur with individual therapists are usually based on the above-mentioned issues: Did you shower this week? Do you have food and shelter? Do you have natural supports to help you? At points, if therapists are lucky, they can actually work with clients on self-regulation of symptoms and teach them skills. However, so much of baseline care is just determining whether they are currently safe.

Then, between those med checks and therapy appointments, a whole lot of things happen. Again, the avalanche falls sometimes slowly and sometimes very rapidly.

On the mental health side of systems of care, we are missing the holistic opportunities. And on the physical health side of systems of care, we are also missing holistic opportunities to work with mental health care providers. We all dream of a day when centers will have all modalities of care available. Steps toward that currently in the works. It's just slow.

Picture this: Imagine it's 2025, just a few years later than now. As a society, we now include in people's care a primary care physician, a nurse, a Reiki specialist, a licensed therapist, a licensed social worker, a spiritual counselor or pastor, and a music, art, and dance therapist. I am not saying these programs don't already exist at some capacity, but in my vision this is occurring more often than not.

People with severe mental illness would be more inclined to attend spiritual coaching sessions or yoga sessions than to go to traditional therapy alone. They would stay more involved if these opportunities were available to them. Right now, people with severe mental illness are conditioned to believe that "this care is as good as it gets." I show up for my meds, maybe chat a little while with my therapist, and that's it. The rest of me is aching inside for more, but this is all that is available to me due to the system, politics, mental health laws, insurance politics, lack of funding issues, and other reasons.

Envision a new level of healing and all the possibilities it could provide to the population suffering from mental illness! If we could speak to their physical, mental, and spiritual health all at once, imagine the hope they would feel. They would feel more included, less stigmatized, more welcomed, and less "crazy." And every human on this planet deserves that level of care regardless of race, socioeconomic status, or religious or cultural differences.

Yet, right now, only the privileged can get access to more specialized holistic care, as insurance companies don't cover these opportunities or recognize them as "evidence based." So if you have extra money because you work a full-time job and don't come from a family of poor economic status, you can schedule yourself a Reiki session or holistic session of some kind on your own dime. Other individuals who would also benefit from access to this are the 5.6 percent of US adults who experience serious mental illness—those 14.2 *million* people—and their families ("Mental Health by the Numbers" 2022). And those are just the individuals with *severe* mental illness.

In the United States, 8.4 million people provide care to an adult with a mental or emotional health issue. They spend an average of thirty-two hours per week providing unpaid care ("Mental Health by the Numbers" 2022). Read that again—thirty-two hours per week is the average amount of time family members spend taking care of loved ones. Imagine systems of care, family sessions, and groups based on holistic wellness for this population alone.

We could be supporting both the individual and the family members together in so many ways that could be more beneficial for the collective whole—for the entire society, causing an enormous ripple effect. If the 22.6 million total Americans mentioned above had access to more holistic care, it would reduce the overall economic impact on the country, reduce homelessness, and increase the vibration of love for the planet.

You may sense my agitation and irritation in my writing due to my own personal experiences and bearing witness to my mother's. Yet I have also seen this with clients repeatedly. They get frustrated with the system as it stands now. They don't always feel valued, understood, seen, or heard by our system. If we address that underlying issue, the pattern, the whole thing could be a game changer. If people feel loved, seen, valued, and heard, they keep coming back. That cliché of "People remember how you make them feel" has meaning in our mental health system. If we treat people who have mental illness with anything less, they don't keep coming, they get defeated, and they give up. *We can do better.*

I want to be clear. Amazing helpers are everywhere. My personal anger is not aimed at any therapists, social workers, psychiatrists, nurses, or doctors of any kind. The frustration is directed at the system. Plenty of centers, therapists, and providers are doing amazing work every day.

I didn't personally get to access any of those wonderful helpers during my mother's decline, though. I had access to my wonderful individual therapist. However, due to my mother's not believing she was ill and her resistance to any help, we couldn't access the other helpers.

The most holistic care that she, and I, received was during the last couple months of her life, with her amazing, caring hospice team. That was the first time in our journey that I saw and bore witness to a whole team of people full of nothing but compassion and understanding. In fact, they had to put me in my place at times when I would get wound up about her symptoms. They did so compassionately.

A cute example of this, quickly: During the last two weeks of my mother's life, she had a different theme to her hallucinations. I noticed things change from her old themes of real estate, money investments, and the like.

One night, she got up in the middle of the night and was walking around the house aimlessly, asking, "Where are the robins? Where are the baby birds?" I thought, *Hmm, this is new.* The next day, I talked to her hospice chaplain about my frustration with her walking around at night and waking me up, and I mentioned that her "hallucinations are getting on my nerves." The chaplain humbled me and talked about the symbolism of robins. He kindly reminded me that I have two parakeets in my home that tweet, so it wouldn't be unreasonable for her to believe there were birds in my home. I was humbled quickly. A side note: the robin is a symbol of rebirth. She talked about these robins the closer to her passing.

Besides illustrating the general issues in the mental health system, I want to share how my mother's cancer diagnosis and treatment are related to her mental health care.

In an earlier story, I mentioned that she had gone to the hospital because her hallucinations were telling her something was wrong with her body. It turned out to be manifestations of her cancer, but her hallucinations thought otherwise. The point of that story is that, due to mental health laws, professionals let someone struggling with cancer and psychosis leave the building without arranging for aftercare.

There are many stories of how her physical health could have been treated differently along her journey, as well. Her physical health was declining because she forgot the dates of appointments or was not aware of what day it was due to her psychosis.

In general, the oncology department she went to did not have programs for mental health. At the end, someone in a new social worker position extended an olive branch to me when my mother kept missing appointments, yet that was right before she was hospitalized. This is another example of the importance of holistic care across medical settings. I don't bring it up to talk negatively about her oncologist's office, as they were wonderful to her in general.

How Others View Mental Health

Those of us who provide caregiving may interact with others across this journey who have different perspectives and reactions to supporting us. Some quick examples (and not an exhaustive list) of some interactions I had with members of the community and loved ones or friends at various times follow.

> The general public (restaurants, etc.): In general, people would stare if they saw her talking to herself or making odd statements to servers.

> Family functions: Some family members would say things such as, "What's wrong with her?" "Is she on drugs?" and "Does she have dementia?" These generally were said out of not understanding the diagnosis but trying to.

> Friends of the caregiver: Friends of mine would say, "Just set boundaries. You don't deserve this. Let her figure things out and help herself." They cared for me and were trying to help.

> Friends of the person who has an illness: Friends of the person with mental illness will typically just shy away from them quietly since they don't know how to help

and the symptoms can be uncomfortable and cause rifts in relationships. Friends of the sick person feel helpless.

Nurses at hospitals and other institutions: I once had a nurse in an emergency room walk my mother back to the hospital bed while stating in front of her, "I'm putting this one in the psych room."

My ultimate favorite is, "Can't she just control it?"

People understand things only from their own levels of perception or their own life experiences. If they've never eaten chocolate cake, then they don't know what it tastes like, right? That doesn't mean they don't have empathy or are horrible human beings. It's just pure ignorance about mental health or psychosis. This is not something taught in general education.

I often wonder how I would respond to a person with schizophrenia had I not had a direct relationship with someone who did or if I weren't a counselor. I would respond in fear also, as others have. When we don't understand or know about something, we fear it. Uncertainty and the unknowns suck.

I could continue with more of what others said or how they reacted. However, my supports and family members were only trying to help me along the way and say things they thought I needed to hear. And truth be told, when friends would say, "You need to set boundaries," they were probably right at that time. But you know my theory on the whole boundary thing by now. Yet my friends' and family's intentions were always pure—to just help. And all the friends and family she had were grieving her loss too. They had lost their dear friend and loved one and all the possibilities and memories of their relationships with her. My mom had an amazing group of friends.

I just humbly ask on behalf of all those who suffer with severe mental illness or psychosis that people always respond with kindness rather than fear. Usually, they are just as scared to interact as you may be or worried about judgment. Show compassion. If you see someone walking down the street talking to themselves, try not to judge them. Try to understand that they are going through a large internal battle that has nothing to do with you.

In addition, I was just angry for a very long time, so accepting help and love from others was a struggle. I have nothing but gratitude for the ones who helped me along the way.

I wish I could go into more depth regarding the caregiver's helpers—the ones helping the caregiver behind the scenes. They are the caregivers of the caregiver. I will just state that I am grateful for mine. I was lucky to have my father and stepmother to support me along the way. The domino effect of mental illness on all families is real.

Moment of Reflection

1. What are some positive experiences you have had in receiving services from outpatient levels of care for severe mentally illness?
2. What have been some experiences that could have been handled better by the system, providers, and others in this journey?
3. What ways did your treatment team members make you feel seen, valued, and heard?
4. What ways did your treatment team or the system make you feel unseen, unvalued, and unheard?
5. In what ways do you wish the system were different?
6. What suggestions would you give to a panel of people designing future programs to better serve the whole person?
7. What programs would you want available to you as the loved one or caregiver?
8. What experiences have you had with loved ones or friends supporting you that felt helpful or hurtful?
9. What is something you long for from your friends and family supporting you?
10. What is something you were grateful for from others helping you in the process?

3

Compassionate Reframing and Boundaries

Thus far in this book, we have explored stories of caring for loved ones and issues in the mental health care system. This chapter has two aims: to assist you in seeing beyond the symptoms of people's illnesses to see them for who they truly are at a soul level, and to provide some ideas for boundaries that you need for yourself in the caregiving process.

To keep yourself out of the constant anger, irritation, or resentment of a loved one helps to strip away those symptoms and see their personality traits for your own understanding and healing—and for the sake of your relationship with your loved one. In addition, it helps to prevent your losing your own sanity in the process of caregiving. Boundaries are needed at certain times and are ever fluctuating.

It is a constant, delicate balancing act of compassion for your loved one and compassion for yourself to maintain your own sense of sanity.

How to Separate the Person from the Illness

Separating the person from the illness as a technique to engender empathy may seem obvious, logical, and like a no-brainer. However, in moments when anger, frustration, and rage take you over while caring for someone with mental illness, it can be quite difficult. There were moments when I said, "I hate her," instead of "I hate this illness."

A more compassionate viewpoint is helpful not only for the person you love but for yourself, to maintain being centered. Sometimes we confuse those symptoms and emotional dysregulation as their personality traits, as if to say "They are just being an asshole or selfish."

For example, my mother was emotionally absent for most of my life. She was in her own world. She was fun, vibrant, and kind. However, she wasn't emotionally present most of the time. This wasn't because she didn't want to be. This was because a myriad of other things were going on inside of her mind, so she couldn't be.

In your caregiving experience, or through loving someone with severe mental illness, have you ever thought, *Wow, they are being a real jerk*? Was it hard for you to discern between symptoms of the person's illness and their personality?

Here's an exercise. Get a blank sheet of paper, and make two columns. On the left side of the paper, write all of the positive qualities you see in the person you love. What makes them unique and special? On the right side of the paper, write all the symptoms of the illness the person has.

Personality Traits	Symptoms of the Illness
• Resilient	• Emotionally absent
• Perseverance	• Stuck in fight-or-flight mode
• Resourceful	• Selfishness
• Caring/kind	• Impulsive
• Giving	• Reactive
• Humorous	• Hallucinations
• Fun	• Delusions
• Hard working	• Disorganization
• Dedicated	• Dysregulation
• Determined	• Flighty
• Active/healthy	• Clumsy
• Great cook	• Irresponsible
• Intelligent	• Forgetfulness

Was your list easy or difficult to make?

Some characteristics on either side seem conflicting, such as "caring/kind" versus "selfishness." How can someone have both traits? Well, there is overlap, of course. My mother could do things of super sweet nature one day and then be incredibly selfish the next day, as if she were a different person. And that is what drove me batshit crazy at times. Those were the moments of confusion and instability in which it was hard to find empathy. However, when we remind ourselves that the symptoms are the mask of the disease or illness and there is a soul underneath all of that, it is easier to have compassion to get through the day-to-day. I would make a mantra for myself and repeat it in my head: "That's not her acting this way right now. It's the illness. Have compassion or take a break. It's not her, it's not her, it's not her."

Here are some questions to ask yourself in moments of frustration with symptoms:

1. What behavior or event am I upset about in this moment?
2. Was the behavior part of who that person is or part of the illness?
3. Since I am upset about an unmet need I have, what else can I still do to get that need met?

For example, one of my situations is below:

1. What behavior or event am I upset about in this moment?

   Example: I was talking to my mother about my divorce, and I really needed her to be there. While I was pouring my heart out, her hallucinations started up and she couldn't focus on our talk. I longed for her advice and support.

2. Was the behavior part of who that person is or part of the illness?

   Example: The hallucinations were part of the illness, not who she is. She cannot control them.

3. Since I am upset about an unmet need I have, what else can I still do to get that need met?

   Example: A. Talk to a different support person.

   B. Continue to accept that my need in this way cannot be met in the way I want it to or that it used to be.

   C. Reframe it. "I can still get other needs met within the relationship. I can still have general companionship with my mother, hang out, watch movies, eat meals, play games."

And, yes, her symptoms may still be present in these other activities. However, the distraction of a game or a movie would subdue the symptoms temporarily. These activities would make her feel love and belonging also, and thus engaged.

This does not mean your feelings of frustration are not valid, or not allowed to exist. They are very much present and real. It's just a method to get through those moments of rage when symptoms interrupt needs that we have in our relationships with those with severe mental illness. It's about finding new, creative ways to still feel connected to the person you love.

There are days as caregivers or loved ones when we just literally cannot do it. Earlier in the book, I mentioned about boundaries being different across time and space, and symptoms. And that is why it is so difficult to write a list of boundaries. Balance is needed in any relationship.

Many types of boundaries exist: time, intellectual, material, sexual, physical, and emotional. It's up to you to determine the ones that matter at the time you are assessing whether you need them.

In couples or marriage counseling, we talk about priorities with clients. The order is religion/spirituality (if you have one), self, your spouse, your children, then work, then everyone and everything else after that. The idea is that if we can't take care of ourselves first, we cannot tend to our marriages or relationships, our children, our work, or anything else. Things become unbalanced, and that results in unmet needs across relationships. The same holds true for any caregiver of mental health. "We have to take care of ourselves, before anyone else." The old cliché rings true every time.

Now, here are some questions you can ask yourself before deciding whether each day is a day when you can put things aside for your loved one.

1. How much stress do I have today as an individual, in my own life (finances, work, other relationship priorities, health, etc.)? Rate it on a 1–10 scale.

Depending on how you answer that, use this as a general way to identify whether you should help the person today.

1–5 = Feel okay, good to go help

6–8 = Pretty stressed out, better consider going another day

9–10 = Danger zone. I will end up lashing out at the person today, so I am not going to go help.

2. Have my general, basic life needs been met today, such as food to eat, bills paid, kids fed, pets okay and fed, and so on? Do I have any of my own appointments to attend to? Is helping the person today going to set me back in my own basic survival needs?

   If my needs are met, then great, I may help. If not, I need to check in with myself on what I need.

3. If I do not help the person today, will I be able to sleep tonight? Or will I remain awake in guilt and shame because I did not help the person?

   Again, you could use a rating scale similar to the one above to rate your level of guilt for not helping.

4. How is this decision to help or not help today impacting my beliefs, values, or spirituality?

5.   Are their basic needs met, or are they in crisis?

This is an example of an answer to number four:

A.   Being a kind person, daughter, and family member means being there for them in time of need. I want to help family when I can.
B.   Being a helper in general is my value. I should help when I can.
C.   Yet I also value my own self-care, my own need for space, and my own right to relax.

ACT (Acceptance and Commitment Therapy) provides a comprehensive sixty word list of values. You can find the full list on their website, ACT Mindfully.com.

The list ranges from A to Z and includes values such as; acceptance, adventure, caring, compassion, connection, encouragement, freedom, flexibility, forgiveness, honesty, independence, love, patience, reciprocity, safety, self-awareness, trust and more. It is a wonderful tool for exploring your primary values in general, and you can utilize this tool and apply it when considering your caregiving journey and boundary setting.

It's important to note that there are no right or wrong answers to these questions. Some weeks, you may feel you can help for ten hours, while other weeks you may feel you can help zero. All that matters is that you feel you are in line with what you need as an individual while simultaneously caring for another human. I also realize that, if you are a parent of a child with a mental illness who is in your care, you may not have these options. It would require additional and potentially paid help to get the self-care time or break you need. I recognize that and see how hard it is for so many parents to get a reprieve.

It is also about acceptance of the fact that things will not always be in alignment. It's acceptance that, some days, you are going to feel 0 percent in alignment with yourself as a caregiver and individual, and some days you'll feel 100 percent in alignment. Other days will be everything in between. If you accept that, your suffering decreases.

Later in the book, I will discuss balancing energy levels and other self-care and healing tips. I'll expand on boundaries more at that time. But I think when people are looking for a book on boundaries as they relate to mental health, they are also looking for *permission* to have boundaries. You have it, you have permission, and you should give that to yourself if needed.

Moment of Reflection

1. Do you feel you can allow yourself to say no or set a boundary from time to time?
2. Do you have any values or beliefs that would keep you from saying no or allowing boundaries?

4

Understanding Grief

Grief is not linear. You have likely heard this statement repeatedly. Grief is a cycle, not a step-by-step process. You have probably also heard, "We don't get through our grief; we grow around it." Mental illness causes us to lose the person we love, or part of that person, and that triggers a grief response within us. Furthermore, that grief response is messy. We bob and weave between many stages of it—sometimes day to day, week to week, or hour to hour. This chapter aims to explore types of grief that may be pertinent to your experience of caring for a loved one with mental illness.

The seven stages of grief are highlighted below for general reference. These stages mostly apply to the loss of loved ones through their passing or death. Yet, we can also apply them to obtaining any medical diagnosis for ourselves or our loved ones or any kind of a loss ("7 Stages of Grief" 2020).

1. Shock and Denial: We react to learning of a loss or diagnosis with disbelief. We feel mourning, sadness, confusion, and discomfort.

2. Pain and Guilt: This is when our pain starts to deepen. We may start to feel guilty of things we could have said or done differently with our loved ones. Sadness, guilt, desperation, and feelings of betrayal could surface.

3. Anger and Bargaining: In this stage, we may lash out at others out of frustration with the upcoming or recent loss. We do things to try to bargain just to see that person again.

4. Depression, Reflection, and Loneliness: This is when a long period of sad reflection may occur. During this time, we realize the true impact of the loss. We may feel depression, frustration, and heaviness.

5. The Upward Turn: This is when we start to adjust to life without our loved ones. Depression begins to lift, and we feel lighter. We may start to feel strengthened, motivated, and awakened.

6. Reconstruction and Working Through: This is when we start to become more adjusted to life without our loved ones, back to more practical parts of ourselves, and functioning better overall on a day-to-day basis. We may feel inspired, determined, and refreshed at this stage.

7. Acceptance and Hope: In this stage, we have fully accepted the loss and find ways to look forward to and plan things for the future. We start to anticipate the future looking much brighter and

feel joy and hope. We also feel relaxed, secure, and comforted.

The above terms are outlined for the general loss of a loved one. Yet the stages are also felt at every level when a loved one receive a diagnosis of mental or physical illness. As caregivers for others, we experience these stages in an ongoing manner as they are very cyclic in nature. One of the most challenging parts of caring for another human being facing any medical challenge in life is anticipatory grief.

Anticipatory Grief

Anticipatory grief, "also referred to as anticipatory loss or preparatory grief, is the distress a person may feel in the days, months or even years before the death of a loved one or other impeding loss" (Conrad 2021).

There is also this heavy anticipation of symptoms of mental illness that occurs for caregivers and loved ones of those who suffer with mental illness.

I have envisioned the anticipation of my mother's mental illness symptoms as many things in my mind over time. Waiting for her voices to come out, waiting for the next crisis to occur—I knew it was coming, and I continued to ask myself, *What's next?* My mind began to paint pictures of and catastrophize her symptoms, based on both logical and irrational thought patterns.

In anticipatory grief of symptoms, your body, mind, and spirit are dysregulated. It's a state of constant hypervigilance that cannot easily be put into words. Your body's baseline is hypervigilance. You can feel through a very whole-body, sensory experience the impending doom that awaits.

To illustrate this, I want to provide a few examples. At one point, my mother had run out of money for the month. She did not have a dollar to her name. She called me while I was at work and begged me to take her dinner from a fast-food restaurant. I was in sessions giving therapy at that moment. She was crying, hysterical, hungry, and begging. I had seen this coming in the week or two prior, and I had made attempts to help her save her money and redirect how she was spending. However, she didn't listen. But that anticipation period was heavy. I knew the ball would drop eventually and I would have to run to her assistance. And so I did.

The buildup to this during the preceding two weeks, my body felt anxious. I felt uptight, unable to focus as much as normal, fearful of what was to come, and unregulated. My mind said, *This is absolutely fucking ridiculous. I hate this situation. I am annoyed with her because she doesn't listen.* My spirit said, *Go help her so she lives and has food.* And I did so, begrudgingly. When I got there, my actions said, *Here, take your food. I left work early to bring you this because you don't listen to me when I try to help.*

The body, mind, and spirit do not act in alignment with who we are as people in times such as these. It is a constant state of internal argument, disarray, and dissonance. *Misalignment* means we do not feel as one with who we are in mind, body, and spirit. And it doesn't f--king feel good.

This feeling resurfaced for several years, over and over and over again. I probably experienced anticipation of my mother's symptoms over a thousand times in small or minor ways and also in larger, more impactful ways. Thus, I lived in a hypervigilant plane of existence for eight years—doing the basics, showing up for work, getting through life, but not really living it. My entire purpose in writing this book is to help you not to do that. I was able to function in my life enough to meet my basic needs, but I felt little to no joy during that time period. And I am betting that most readers can relate with this.

The trick is self-regulation, self-compassion, and working from our heart chakras to get through these overwhelming, whole-body, -mind, and -spirit issues as they arise through our caregiving experiences. That is the only way to stay aligned with who you are, hold your authenticity as a person in this process, and keep your sanity.

So when I say I am not perfect, I surely am not. I acted well enough to get my mom and myself through some things during these eight years. But at many times I begrudgingly did things that I didn't want to do and thus acted negatively toward her.

Ambiguous Loss

Ambiguous loss is another type of grief and loss. The term was coined by Dr. Pauline Boss in the 1970s. Ambiguous loss differs from anticipatory grief. *Ambiguous loss* is defined as "a relational disorder caused by lack of facts surrounding the loss of a loved one. It is not individual pathology because the problem emerges from the outside context and not the psyche. Ambiguous loss differs from ordinary loss in that there is no verification of death, or no certainty that the person will come back to return to the way they used to be" (Ambiguous Loss 2022).

Boss defines two different types of ambiguous loss. The first is when a loved one is physically absent but has a psychological presence. This means that a loved one is physically missing, or their body is gone. Examples of this are situations such as divorces, adoptions, and loss of physical contact with family. A more specific example would be, *I miss my ex-spouse and all the potential joy we could have had together.* The ex-spouse still exists, yet you are grieving the loss of what could have been, the visions you painted in your mind of what could have happened differently or better in the marriage.

The second type of ambiguous loss is when a loved one is psychologically absent but physically present. This loved one is emotionally, cognitively, or psychologically absent while being physically there. Examples of this include dementia, chronic illness, and mental illness.

So in terms of my experience of ambiguous loss, I can relate to the second type due to my mother's emotional and cognitive absence. I experienced the loss of who she was without those symptoms, and I missed the potential that my mother had to be a mother. I missed all those times that didn't happen, when she would have been emotionally present in our conversations and supported me emotionally at big moments in life. I missed the mom I thought I would have had for the bulk of my adult years—the one dancing in stilettoes, having fun, and cooking delicious meals.

The seven stages of grief can also be applied to your feelings of having a family member with a mental illness. Below is how I experienced these stages at various points. Then, at the end of the section, you can reflect on how you have experienced them.

Shock and Denial:

- Getting her diagnosis of schizophrenia and feelings of disbelief
- Getting her cancer diagnosis and feelings of shock
- Shock in regard to the way the system treated her
- Shock in the way others treated her at times (friends, family)

Pain and Guilt:

- Caregiver guilt
- Pain of not being able to help her due to mental health laws

- Feeling pain due to the emotional absence of my mother
- Pain in regard to the way other people treated her

Shame and Fear:

- Fear that I would find her dead in her apartment
- Fear of her going to court to file charges based on her hallucinations and delusions
- Fear of rejection from others—for herself and me (others won't understand; they will judge)
- Fear of my getting diagnosed eventually with late-onset schizophrenia
- Fear of abandonment because of the situation and others' initial responses
- Shame and embarrassment for the ways her symptoms presented in front of others, causing me to try to redirect her symptoms so people wouldn't judge
- Shame in my own behavior and responses to her at times out of frustration
- Shame that I was a horrible person for having these feelings of frustration
- Fear that she would never be "present" with me in the moment because of her illness, that I would never have her back
- Fear that she would never get treatment

Anger and Bargaining:

- Resentment toward her: *How can she not see what she is doing? How can she be so damn selfish? How come she cannot control her symptoms?*

o Anger about not being able to talk to her and feeling it was a one-sided relationship: *Can you just listen to me for once?*

o Anger every time her symptoms presented

o Anger for trying to shield or protect her when she didn't want it or need it

o Anger toward God: *Why would he do this to a person?*

o Bargaining with God: *If you help with this, I promise X.*

Depression, Isolation, and Loneliness:

o Feeling isolated and depressed that I couldn't talk to others about it

o Feeling isolated because I didn't know anyone who had a loved one with schizophrenia

o Feeling isolated because, when I did talk to others about her symptoms, their response was, "She can control herself and make her own decisions" because they didn't know what to say

o Losing myself in the whole process

Spouse's Grief:

My mother's ex-husband (my stepfather), Ron, had written a synopsis on his experiences of loving and being married to someone with a severe mental illness. And in his story were a lot of details of their life together, some that are meant to be kept private. However, he was generous and forthcoming about the grief and loss he faced alone for many years. He wanted to provide some relatable points for the spouses out there. The section below was written with information he provided.

Ron's Viewpoint

Grief, Loss, and Struggles Ron Faced

Ron as a spouse can relate with all the stages of grief mentioned above and the ambiguous loss. He wished he could have done simple things with my mother that couples do. He longed to be able to take her to the movie theater, attend friends' parties and more social gatherings of friends they once shared, and other things that we take for granted at times. He couldn't take her to those places, as her symptoms would manifest out loud and cause distress for both of them. He longed to see her dancing in her stilettoes like no one was watching, just like the day he met her.

They had a great, loving relationship for many years prior to her symptoms and the avalanche falling. Ron felt ambiguous loss for all these missed opportunities in their marriage, these moments of connection with each other, friends, and loved ones. Their emotional and physical intimacy dissipated many years ago. He longed to connect with her. The life they had prior to her symptoms was gone. He was now in a whole new life of living in isolation from support and trying to keep his head above water.

The hardest part for Ron was that my mother's symptoms of psychosis and the themes associated with them were about him. This was an added layer of difficulty. I mentioned earlier that she had aggressed toward him at times. Yet I also said that people with mental illness are not typically aggressive. Ron did have relational trauma because of this—because of her symptoms, not her. The symptoms were the problem, not her.

Besides the emotional losses, he experienced financial struggles, hardship, and loss. Having a spouse with severe mental illness can be very costly. Over the years, he spent several thousands of dollars managing her health care or other issues that arose due to her symptoms. He experienced the same frustration that I did about the mental health system and laws but at an earlier period in her life.

Lessons Ron Learned

He shared that he had guilt about wishing he could have done things differently at times—wishing he could have gotten her treatment sooner or that he would have reached out to others for support sooner and more often. These are the lessons he wishes to share:

- Don't wait to reach out to other loved ones and family members for support.
- Don't wait to reach out for support and help professionally; reach out when you start noticing symptoms.
- Being a spouse of someone with severe mental illness exposes you to the whole array of human

emotions: fear, worry, anxiety, depression, sadness, grief, and heartache of every kind.

- Seek support from others through support networks and online resources from others experiencing the same.
- Remember to engage in self-care throughout the process and allow yourself not to feel guilt for that.
- Work through any fears you may have about what other people think of mental illness. You are not alone.

Overall, Ron's process of healing involved looking at the ways he carried this alone in isolation for a long time. He made decisions that he thought were best at the time he was making them and did so the best way he knew how at that time. He reports that he has worked through that grief and is working on forgiving himself.

As for me, I didn't really feel the other three stages of grief—the upward turn, reconstructing and working through, and acceptance and hope—until after Mom's passing, so I will get into those in the second part of the book. However, the shift upward of having a loved one with mental illness and accepting it is also a cyclic endeavor.

A few things did help me accept her diagnosis. I wrote earlier about how to accept the person as they are and separate the person from the illness and symptoms. Even as a professional in the field, I struggled with this at times. As I continued to try to work through my frustrations with her symptoms, the number-one thing I came back to was "loving her spirit." Furthermore, I had to remember that all those voices, hallucinations, and delusions were not her. It's just that it got so bad that it was hard to see her spirit shining through sometimes.

Moment of Reflection

1. What of the seven stages have you experienced in your journey with mental health or caring for someone with mental health?
2. Which stages have you not yet experienced?
3. What types of anticipation grief have you experienced?
4. In what ways have you experienced ambiguous loss?
5. Can you relate with anything specifically listed in my personal account of the stages of grief?
6. What other events or situations were challenging for you?
7. Where were you in your life when you got the diagnosis for your loved one? Where were you mentally, emotionally, physically, and spiritually? What age?

PART TWO

Apples

5

Introduction to Apples

We have looked so far at what it's like to love someone with mental illness. Now this section is about you, the caregiver. We've all heard the phrase, "The apple doesn't fall far from the tree." In this chapter, we will explore your own fears and worries about your mental health, finding purpose in the pain and journey of caring for a loved one, and spirituality as part of the healing process.

How much have you questioned your own sanity in the process of loving someone else with mental health? Have you ever thought you have a mental illness? Are you suffering with trying to heal generational trauma?

In this part I will be extremely vulnerable in an effort to help others. This isn't a story I am proud of telling. I have diagnosed myself with many conditions that the DSM-5 has listed over the course of the last decade or so. (The

DSM-5 is a main resource that practitioners in the mental health field use to diagnose patients.)

I theorized that I had everything from a personality disorder to an anxiety disorder and major depressive disorder. I tried to fit myself in various boxes many times. In fact, I went to three different licensed professionals at various points asking if I had one of these diagnoses. And, of course, I even thought I could be "pre-schizophrenic." All three of those licensed professionals told me no. In fact, my last therapist got sick of my asking and thinking I was schizophrenic and asked me, "Do you want to be?"

Furthermore, the therapists told me that I was constantly trying to adjust to the trauma of having a loved one with mental illness and, of course, other personal life factors outside of my mother's mental illness. I eventually stopped asking and accepted their response.

I used to even chew gum when I went into public places because I became paranoid that I was talking to myself, even though I was not. I had a significant fear of "getting schizophrenia" at one point because of being so neurotically wrapped up in it. I thought, *I better chew my gum. I don't want my internal thoughts coming out in front of others.* This was earlier in the process, when I was burnt out and feeling too surrounded by my mother's condition.

Schizophrenia can be hereditary in that, if you have a loved one with the diagnosis, your odds of having mental illness increase. Having one first-degree relative (such as a parent or sibling) with schizophrenia increases your risk by 10 percent, and it increases to 50 percent if both of your parents have the diagnosis. However, there are environmental factors at play as well, such as trauma, drug use, exposure to various toxins or viruses before birth, and immune system diseases. Thus, while the risk percentage for those who have one parent with the illness doesn't seem high, I still was concerned and had difficulty reframing this to decrease my worry.

I realize that not everyone reading this is a child of a person with a mental health disorder, so this may not resonate with everyone reading. If you are not a biological family member of the person you love, you may feel differently in the next few chapters. But even if you are a nonbiological family member, I am sure that at times you have at least questioned your sanity in the process. You may even be someone with severe mental illness.

I have suffered from clinical levels of self-doubt, self-esteem issues, self-loathing and self-hatred behaviors, indecision, fear of abandonment, fear of rejection, obsessiveness, anxiety, and depression, among others. I suffered from overidentification with mental illness. I worked full time in the mental health field for thirteen years, studied it for seven, and walked in it daily with my mother. It was like I was stuck in this bubble and couldn't breathe. Everything I did, I questioned. Every. Single. Thing. It could have been about what exercise I would do that day or general anxiety about time. The list is immensely long. And, again, as I mentioned in earlier chapters, I wasn't living, or felt I wasn't. I wasn't enjoying my life.

We categorize aspects of mental health into boxes in the DSM-5. They are useful and offer a basic guideline for understanding human behavior. Yet we get wrapped up too tightly in diagnosing others or diagnosing ourselves. Even this generation growing up now is keenly aware of mental health. I have children and adolescents coming into my office telling me what their diagnoses are. While awareness of mental health is a positive step forward in our culture, it's also a setback. We are overidentifying everything we do as the result of a mental health condition instead of just a natural progression of human existence. (Not to discount decades of research and validity.)

I want to be clear before sharing more personal details that I do not blame my mother for my "issues." Not all of one's issues or symptoms are related to parents in general. Our lives are a series of individual and unique experiences, yet with the same underlying core feelings. We all suffer in our own ways as a result of that individual life path.

What I am referring to next is how my individual issues were magnified as a result of having a parent with mental illness. I felt like I was constantly putting my issues under a microscope because of my environment, in which I was constantly surrounded by mental health. I am also talking about healing generational trauma. I want to propose ways for you to heal yourself also so that patterns in generational trauma can be transmuted.

I saw this floating around on social media at some point, and it has stuck with me ever since. The quote is from a piece titled "Become, Become, Become" by John Roedel

(2022). Look it up to read the whole thing. God is talking to the author in this excerpt, and the moral of it is that we are not broken; we are just trying to "unbecome" who or what we are not, shedding the pieces that do not fit us anymore and becoming who God made us to be.

> God: Becoming who I created you to be! A person of light and love and charity and hope and courage and joy and mercy and grace and compassion. I made you for more than the shallow pieces you have decided to adorn yourself with that you cling to with such greed and fear. Let those things fall off of you. I love you! Don't change! Become! Become! Become! Become who I made you to be. I'm going to keep telling you this until you remember it.

It's a beautiful illustration of shedding what is no longer meant for us, letting our souls remain.

And before continuing, I want to define the world *healing*. We all look at this differently. We have different definitions and ideas of what that process looks like. Healing is not linear. We heal from birth until death. And sometimes, the word *healing* itself imposes brokenness. Healing is just part of life.

I will now break down the areas in which I suffered the most, describe how those "symptoms" presented, and allow room for you to reflect also. The three most present for me were fear of abandonment, fear of rejection, and limited self-confidence or self-worth. And interestingly, these three are all very related and part of the trauma response. It took me forever to realize this—or really, I realized it but was stuck in terms of how to change it. I eventually had my aha moment and realized that these were not separate issues but were all related. It's like I wanted to keep picking apart every single flaw and putting myself into categories.

Fear of Abandonment

I had a fear that people would leave me. This changed over the years and across different relationships and romantic partnerships. Some of the ways it manifested was through my choosing to run from relationships before others could run from me. I did this multiple times, and specifically to two long-term romantic relationships. It was a vicious cycle for decades. I would attach to things that were not healthy for me also because I didn't want to be alone. I sought safety and security in not being alone. It created codependency-related behaviors.

The root cause to this was feeling abandoned by a parent who suffered from mental illness when I was a child. It was also because of other circumstantial things across my life span, such as other relationships, instability in upbringing, and my own life choices.

Fear of Rejection

I had a fear that people didn't like me, thought I was weird, and considered me not good enough. I would keep myself from doing things I was passionate about because of that fear of rejection. I held myself back from my goals as a result—professionally, personally, and relationally. I also suffered from body-image issues and feared others thought I was fat.

The root cause to this was feeling that I had not been good enough to get the attention I wanted and needed as a child from a parent with a mental illness. And, of course, other factors from my life came into play as well.

Limited Self-Worth or Self-Doubt

I had a debilitating level of self-doubt and felt like I was never good enough. It would present itself as people-pleasing behaviors, seeking attention and external validation through others in various ways.

The root cause of that was, again, not feeling good enough to get the emotional fulfillment I needed as a child, coupled with a life span of interactions with others and life circumstances. Of course, also, being told by society that I had to be a certain way influenced me. We all have experienced this.

All of those inner-child wounds carried throughout my life, and I just kept adding to them by making some of the same mistakes over and over again. I am not shaming myself by stating that. Healing takes the time it takes for each of us individually. And we are constantly healing.

Are there other areas in which you feel pain? If so, what are they?

Fear of abandonment, fear of rejection, and low self-worth are common problems across humanity. We all suffer from them; it's more of a spectrum of intensity. No one likes any of that. But we all feel these things across different life domains at various points in our lives. And societal expectations in our country don't help either.

What is the common factor among caregivers for people with mental illness or their family members? It is the underlying root of where they came from: feeling that lack of emotional availability of a parent or loved one. If you are a parent caring for a child, a spouse caring for your spouse, or other caregiver, I hope you were able to sit still, reflect on and relate to these questions, and consider how they are related to being a caregiver of someone who is severely mentally ill.

The Inner Child

As children, we get messages from our caregivers or parents regarding whether people are safe or not, if they can be trusted. If we don't feel safe, those fears we discussed can arise, as well as many others.

Other examples of symptoms of childhood wounds, specifically in relation to emotional neglect, can include a deep feeling that something is wrong with you, being a people pleaser, not being able to let go of situations and people, heightened anxiety over something new, feeling guilty for setting boundaries, driven to be an overachiever or a perfectionist, having problems starting or completing tasks, exhibiting constant self-criticism, feeling ashamed to express emotions, being ashamed of your body, having a deep distrust of others, and avoiding conflict at all costs.

The symptoms can cause insecurity and anxiety in adulthood and manifest in our relationships with others across home, work, and other life domains. They can cause intense suffering and self-sabotaging behaviors.

My inner child needed and yearned for the emotional presence of her parents. Her basic needs and wants were met (fed, clothed, taken care of, supported in some ways), but she longed for consistency, stability, and emotional presence. She also liked to try to heal dying animals (butterflies), liked to play doctor with family and friends, and knew she wanted to be a healer.

So many free resources are available online with journal prompts for inner-child healing. A simple internet search will give you many freebies!

As adults, we all have these inner childhood wounds that we carry around in our daily lives. They are acted out in scenarios on a subconscious level, and we don't even realize they are until we do the shadow work. Shadow work is seeing the parts of yourself that are "hidden" (Jeffrey 2022).

My inner child made me a "wounded healer." And I found purpose in my pain, not only from my childhood but also from having to care for someone who was directly related to my inner wounds as an adult. We all can find purpose in our pain. My shadow work included healing my inner child, healing my relationship with my mother and others in general, forgiveness, and much more.

What has healing looked like for you? How do you define *healing*?

I truly am not creative enough to develop my own cool quotes about healing. However, I am smart enough to do an internet search and plug a quote into this section of the book.

"To heal is to touch with love that which we previously touched with fear." —Stephen Levine

Healing is not linear. Healing is a lifelong venture, as we always have something to move through.

Finding Purpose in Your Pain

Have you seen the TikTok trend of people lying outside in the grass and God whispering, "Your pain wasn't for nothing. It was all for something"? I love TikTok. It is a magically creative place for humanity. Anyway, there is purpose in our pain.

> Your lovely soul was created for a divine
> purpose. To show your incredible beauty
> to the world, to rejoice in the grace that

surrounds you always, and to simply love beyond the end of time. — Robert Clancy

In *The Purpose Driven Life*, author Rick Warren (2002) states,

> God intentionally allows you to go through painful experiences to equip you for ministry to others. The Bible says, "He comforts us in all our troubles so that we can comfort others." When others are troubled, we will be able to give them the same comfort God has given us.
>
> If you really desire to be used by God, you must understand a powerful truth: the very experiences that you have resented or rejected most in life—the ones you wanted to hide and forget—are the experiences God wants to use to help others. They are your ministry.
>
> For God to use your painful experiences, you must be willing to share them. You have to stop covering them up, and you must honestly admit your faults, failures and fears. (p. 247)

He further talks about "determining your shape" for serving God: "You will be most effective when you use your spiritual gifts and abilities in the areas of your heart's desire, and in a way that best expresses your personality and experiences."

If you haven't read this book, go get it!

I tried to fight the idea that this subject matter of families with severe mental illness was my "shape," my ministry, or my purpose for a while. I didn't want schizophrenia to be a topic I regularly discussed. I resented the illness. But here I am, at age thirty-nine, and I have been a counselor in the field for over a decade while also simultaneously loving someone with it. I can no longer deny it. It hit me in the face over and over. So here I am, ready to support and assist others.

Are you a mother with a child who has a severe mental health condition? If so, does watching the system and access-to-care issues unfold trigger your purpose? Is it watching your child suffer, feeling helpless, and finding the strength to move on? Is it taking all this and telling your story to improve some area of the system, to support other parents, to advocate for something?

Everyone needs you. All of us are struggling with unique yet similar experiences, wanting to hear from you. Your story is important. The various specific trials you went through as a caregiver of someone with mental illness sheds light on the knowledge someone needs to grow and improve. Right now, someone out there is waiting to hear your story to feel connected and supported. And telling your story is so cathartic.

We are not defined by our pain but rather strengthened by it. Our whole identities and life's work don't have to surround our pain. You can give back to your area of knowledge in smaller ways by just helping your community.

To quote Brené Brown from *The Gifts of Imperfection* (as I don't think I could have made it through writing a book without quoting such a therapy goddess), "Owning our story and loving ourselves through that process is the bravest thing we'll ever do" (2010).

Spiritual Awakening

I waivered in deciding how much of or even if I would share this part of my journey. When we start talking about spirituality, people sometimes check out. Yet I feel like this part of the journey is what led ultimately to my healing and freeing myself. So it's worth a share if it somehow helps you.

Another fear is related to delusions of grandeur. I figured that, if I shared this story, people would think I have delusions of being important, high and mighty. Or people will think, *She thinks she is a special one.* In actuality, quite the contrary is the case. Spiritual ego is a real thing. No one is better than another whether they have had an awakening or not. I recently had a conversation with a friend who said she believed she had one years ago but ignored it. Everyone has spiritual gifts that can be tapped into at any time.

I debated for a very long time whether I should tell my mom's story, our story. Cloaked in that fear of rejection, fear of criticism, fear I wouldn't be able to, it wasn't until my spiritual awakening that I felt remotely strong enough to do it or felt I had permission to do it. I kept thinking, *This story is not important. I just think it is because it hits home to me. This story can't help anyone. It's not that rare of a story.* And so many other defeating thoughts.

December 2021 is when my awakening started. I spent the whole year of 2020 self-reflecting, doing shadow work, trying to heal all my attachment wounds from older relationships, and trying to stop repeating cycles of chasing after emotionally unavailable men. It was the "reconstruction and working through" stage of both the loss of my mother and a divorce. I had been chasing emotionally unavailable individuals for a while, and I was repeating some of the same behaviors I was trying not to do.

I had to tell myself "Stop. Regulate yourself." I was searching for love in all the wrong places. Logically, I knew I was making the same choices over again. Emotionally, I kept telling myself justifications of why it was okay to keep doing them. I finally stopped and got myself in check with the help of my wonderful therapist. I then, finally, put myself out there to go on a date with someone I met online. Oh, how the dating world has changed in the last decade or so. But that's a story for another book!

I created an outline of the qualities I wanted in my next relationship and how I was going to find it. It was a checklist of attributes I was looking for in a partner—all those fun things. I had been on one dating site for a few months at this point yet hadn't taken the leap to actually go on a date with someone new. Then I did. I was so nervous, as I hadn't been on a real first date since I was in high school—about twenty years ago. I was nervous leading up to the first date. *OMG what will I wear? What do I talk about? What do I share on a first date and not share?* All the usual worries of the wonderful dating world.

I made some newbie dating errors. I was so excited to feel a new connection with someone and wanted to show that I was a consistent, caring woman. But my old patterns of behavior surfaced. I was trying to prove my worth for fear that someone wouldn't like me or stay. I was still engaging in old behaviors but in much softer ways. I was still trying to be perfect or what I thought the other person wanted or would view as perfect. I was kind, affirming, independent, and caring. I was subconsciously trying to prove my worth, still.

My point in telling this story is that, for the first time in forever, I felt hope. I had never been talked to the way my date talked to me. He made me feel amazing. He made me feel beautiful and smart. I don't remember a time in any of my earlier relationships that I ever felt that way. And to be clear, I did really like him. He met all the criteria on my checklist: charming, smart, goal driven, spiritual, kind, hardworking, and "dreamy." Ultimately, it didn't progress.

But relationships are mirrors, right? They teach us something about ourselves. This one taught me a few things: 1) I am worthy of love and affection. 2) I am beautiful and kind. 3) I can be myself and be loved, even if he (or anyone) didn't want that at that time. 4) Just because he did not choose me, I am not any less worthy of love.

A certain quote resonates with me: "You are so used to your own features, you don't know how beautiful you look to a stranger." I spent thirty-nine years thinking I was an ugly duckling, suffering from body-image issues and crippling self-doubt. Relationships I had prior to this perpetuated this belief in small but noticeable ways. This very quick encounter with a random person from online dating made that go away.

Directly after this encounter, the holidays came, and on December 27 I had the first undeniable feelings of my awakening. For the whole month of December, I felt like I was floating, and I felt inspired. I was more soft, present, and attuned with what my clients needed to hear from me. It was odd—a shift toward peace inside me.

On December 27, I woke up at 3:33 a.m. Then again, on December 28, I woke at the same exact time. My ears kept ringing. I was seeing synchronicities in numbers and songs. I started having lucid dreams. I felt waves of intense energy from wanting to dance in my kitchen like a raging adolescent full of sexual energy to wanting to sit and write and do shadow work and cry under a blanket.

I saw angel numbers at times I was thinking about various things, and it was too obvious to be a coincidence. I saw other numbers as well, like 1:11, 11:11, 444, 333, and so on.

I felt these were moments of pure unconditional love in my soul and over my entire body, intense waves of feeling loved and supported, of finally feeling like I actually loved myself and felt worthy. I felt inspired and wanted to live authentically as who I am, eliminating blocks in my throat chakra. The fear I had dissipated.

One morning, I woke up with that full-body experience of unconditional love, and a song was playing in my mind: "Somewhere Out There" from the movie *An American Tail* (Ingram 1986). It was a song I had forgotten all about. But when I woke up, I listened to it. I have never cried the way I cried when I listened to this—you know, the whole body-and-soul-existential-speaking-to-your-inner-child cry. For reference, the movie is about a mouse who gets separated from his mother and family, and he meets others on his ventures to search for his family.

> Somewhere out there
> Beneath the pale moonlight
> Someone's thinking of me
> And loving me tonight
>
> Somewhere out there
> Someone's saying a prayer
> That we'll find one another
> In that big somewhere out there

Go listen to the whole song really quick. Then come back.

Did it hit your soul? Are you crying? I am not crying; you are crying! If it didn't affect you that way, that is okay.

But when it came to me out of nowhere, it truly felt like a sign. I felt that my mother and deceased loved ones were sending me a big, lyrical hug. "Love will see us through"—you're damn right it will! But aren't the lyrics so true? We are all love and protected and prayed for.

My desire to write my mom's story, our story, was no longer cloaked in fear. It was like I realized it was okay to tell it, that whatever readers or critics might say didn't matter. My intention in telling it was pure of heart. My big dreams of wanting to not only tell this story but to shift my career into more of this specialty was no longer, in my mind, a delusion of grandeur. It was just a dream I had about which traditional mental-health approaches had made me shame myself for years.

The awakening taught me more of how we all are connected. We all want the same things: to love and be loved; to feel like we belong; to feel valued, seen, and heard. We are all connected and heal one another on an ongoing basis throughout this lifetime. Just as Julia Roberts talked about in the movie *Eat, Pray, Love*, everyone on your journey is a teacher, and if you accept that every person you encounter has a lesson, then you will be abundant in your life.

While my awakening awareness started with a super quick and cryptic romantic story, that wasn't the point. That interaction just triggered my spiritual awakening to unfold. It gave me hope, inspiration, confidence, and a desire to be the best, most authentic version of myself so I can live in purpose and serve others the best way I can. It gave me peace and comfort knowing that deceased loved ones like my mother are watching over me. It also taught me to trust my intuition.

Awakenings have been known throughout history to happen to individuals when they have encountered life traumas. Many books about this exist. Trauma often leads to transformation of the self, identity changes, and new ways of thinking. Some people call awakenings existential crises. Whatever you believe is okay.

When you read on, you will see that a lot of my recommendations for healing are based on spiritual theories. I resonate with theories from spiritual psychology due to my awakening. I hope this helps you too.

But the point of telling you about my awakening is that it's part of the healing process of life. Every soul has spirit guides, angel guides, and deceased ancestors watching after them. They follow you and communicate with you. But humans often don't see them or pay attention to them.

Researchers, philosophers, metaphysics, and others have all studied this. Thus, I am only sharing this as a message of hope since spirituality influenced my healing and is being integrated into my life and work. I am not saying that you must have spirituality in order to heal. I would never impose that on anyone. Yet the reconstruction and working through phases of grief can be supported by spirituality.

In the next chapter, we will review some more healing tools.

Moment of Reflection: Fear of Mental Illness

1. Have you ever felt the need to diagnose yourself?
2. What symptoms do you feel you have had?
3. If you have diagnosed yourself, what was your absolute breaking point?

Moment of Reflection: Fear of Abandonment

1. Can you relate with fear of abandonment, fear of rejection, or limited self-worth or self doubt?
2. If so, from where do you think it originated?
3. In what ways did it present in your life?

Moment of Reflection: Inner Child

1. What does your inner child say and yearn for?
2. When you talk to your inner child, what do they say to you?
3. What are the things you enjoyed as a child?
4. What were the things that scared you most as a child in your family?
5. What was your inner child's viewpoint on life? What is yours now? How are they different or the same?
6. What's one quality of your inner child that you loved but don't possess now?

Moment of Reflection: Purpose in Your Pain

1.   What purpose(s) can you find in your pain?
2.   What lessons are in your pain?
3.   What is your ministry based on your pain?

Moment of Reflection: Spirituality

1.   If you identify with being spiritual, what signs and synchronicities have you encountered?
2.   Have you had moments of pure clarity about your purpose in life?
3.   What experiences have you had that have given you hope in your journey?
4.   What are your spiritual beliefs, if any?

6

Healing Tools

In the last chapter, we discussed fears we have of becoming ill and finding meaning or purpose in our journey of caring for loved ones with mental illness. In this chapter, four tools will be provided to support you in exploring ways to work through the pain: finding forgiveness for ourselves and others; practicing nonattachment; practicing core mindfulness and taking a nonjudgmental approach to our thoughts, feelings, and experiences; and finally externalizing the problem from ourselves. It is a "scrapbook", if you will, of interventions you can choose from that resonate with you, and leave ones that do not.

Intervention 1: Forgiveness of Self, of Others, and of Them

Referring to the stages of grief mentioned earlier, the last three stages of the model include the upward turn, reconstruction and working through, and acceptance and hope. We have spent the first half of this book addressing pain and thinking about our pain. Now it's time to work through healing our pain.

Forgiving ourselves, forgiving others in our journey, and forgiving the person we love with severe mental illness is part of this process. Read mine below and think of what would be helpful for you to forgive for or release.

Forgiveness of Yourself

Identifying what you have to forgive yourself for is step one. This includes matters related to you as a caregiver of your loved one and other unique aspects of yourself (the apples) that you hold onto.

I had to forgive myself for

- all the times I lashed out at my mother for her symptoms,
- all the times I felt selfish and that I could have done more,

- all the times I avoided her because I just "couldn't" that day, even though I knew she just wanted time with me, and
- all the times I hurt others because of my own inner-child wounds and attachment wounds.

Forgiveness of Others

I had to forgive others for

- any statements friends and family may have made about psychosis or mental illness that came from a place of not understanding and
- the mean looks from random people in restaurants or grocery stores us when my mom was symptomatic.

Forgiveness for the Person with Mental Illness

I had to forgive my mother for

- not being emotionally present or available;
- all the times I wanted to talk to her, but she couldn't;
- all the times she got drunk and passed out or got sick; and
- her selfish behaviors over the years (e.g., choosing the bar or a night out over me).

We still have a right to our feelings as they are valid. Yet to heal, we have to let go. I mentioned earlier that people can only love us the best way they know how at the time we are experiencing them. Forgiveness doesn't mean you agree with what happened. It just means you are choosing to let go of the pain so you can heal yourself.

All of my own inner-child wounds and memories became healed once I understood that the issue was the avalanche of her symptoms and not her. Earlier in her life, when I was younger, she didn't yet have psychosis. However, she experienced trauma and addictions before the onset of her psychosis, and what I had to forgive her for was all related to her symptoms. I literally have thought, *She wasn't trying to be an a—hole*, because she wasn't.

I Forgive

So I forgive you, Mom, for all the times I wanted you to be there, but you couldn't. I forgive you for being selfish at times. I forgive you for all the times you got drunk and passed out. I forgive it all, and I release it. It no longer serves my higher good to hold onto any pain or memory from the past. And I will continue to hold love and light in my heart for you always.

I forgive myself for the times I lashed out at you, for the times I felt selfish, and for the times I avoided seeing you. I only loved you the best way I knew how at the time I was with you.

Affirmations for Forgiving and Releasing

I forgive those who have wronged me or my mother and choose to live a life full of love, joy, and peace.

I forgive everyone for all perceived wrongdoings and release them with love.

I see and treat my family through the eyes of love, even if we do not completely agree on everything.

I love and accept my family members for exactly who they are, their souls.

My parents did the best they could. I forgive them and let go of any resentment or grudges I once held toward them.

I forgive the symptoms that my mother faced. I release my anger and resentment toward these symptoms.

These are some quick examples of versions of affirmations for releasing. What affirmations for forgiveness would be helpful for you?

Intervention 2: Nonattachment

Nonattachment is the concept of learning how to let go of the thoughts and emotions that create suffering. It is a principle in Buddhism, which teaches that attachment is the root of all suffering and that expectations of a particular outcome cause suffering. If we remove expectations of outcomes and let things flow, we remove suffering.

An article I read recently (Luna 2022) describes six ways to practice nonattachment.

1. **"Stop looking for happiness in external things."**

   This implies that we look externally for happiness, such as, "I will be happy once I get this job, this house, this money," and so on. When we go internally for happiness, we find peace within.

2. **"Let go of the 'shoulds' and 'musts.'"**

   This speaks to the expectations we put on ourselves and others: "They should help me." "They should be nicer." "I should be rich." "I should be kinder." When we let go of these expectations, we reduce suffering.

3. **"Practice allowing."**

   This is about allowing life to happen as it is. Allow thoughts, feelings, and emotions to just exist. Allowing things to go how they may reduces suffering.

4. **"Make friends with uncertainty."**

   When we are worried about uncertainty, we suffer. We try to plan, control, and predict things and live in anxiety as a result. Letting life unfold naturally reduces this.

5. **"Learn to observe your thoughts and feelings."**

   This implies that, when we assign meaning to our thoughts, it causes suffering. If we don't give our thoughts importance, they cease to cause us pain. Thus, observing our thoughts and feelings and allowing them to flow reduces suffering.

6. **"See how transient all things are."**

Things around us are constantly changing and evolving. Nothing lasts forever. Everything is always naturally flowing and shifting. Accepting the reality of this reduces suffering.

Application of these principles to ourselves in our caregiving experience is helpful. It is also helpful for ourselves as individuals when healing our wounds. The very changes and shifts in this mindset eliminate further suffering.

Example of Application to Caregiving Experience

1. **"Stop looking for happiness in external things."**

Before:

"I won't be happy until this mental health issue is gone."

"I won't be happy until the mental health system changes and takes care of my loved one."

"I won't be happy until I get a break from this role I am in as caregiver."

Instead:

"I determine my own level of happiness and balance through this crisis, through these crises. These things are outside my level of control. I have the power to find happiness and peace within myself through this process."

2. **"Let go of 'shoulds' and 'musts.'"**

Before:

"They should be helping me with my mom more than they are."

"My mom should be nicer to me considering everything I am doing for her."

"I should be kinder than I am."

Instead:

"I let go of these 'shoulds' and 'musts' and allow things to be as they are and accept them as part of human experience. I notice my thoughts yet allow them to pass."

3. **"Practice allowing."**

Before: "I want these feelings and thoughts to stop."

"I want to push them under a rug and forget they exist."

"I am going to pretend these feelings don't exist, avoid them, push them away, or distract myself."

Instead:

"I am just going to allow these symptoms to happen as they may. I release trying to control them and any situations related to them. I am going to allow my thoughts to come and go. I allow this experience to just happen as it's meant to."

4. **"Make friends with uncertainty."**

Before:

"I am afraid every day of the uncertainty and unpredictability of her condition."

Instead:

"I accept that I cannot control the outcome of her condition or the manner in which her symptoms or needs present."

5. **"Learn to observe your thoughts and feelings."**

Before:

"I want to rush through these thoughts and feelings because they are uncomfortable."

Instead:

"I recognize that I have thoughts and feelings about her mental health and symptoms. I see them, and I know they matter. I allow them to exist, and I allow them to be felt and pass through me."

6. **"See how transient things are."**

Before:

"This will last forever—this suffering and pain for her, for me, for us."

Instead:

"This will not last forever, this time period of her life. These difficulties will eventually pass, as hard as it is to see at this time. Things do and will change."

Can you feel it? Could you feel that shift in your body, mind, and soul as you went through that example? Could you feel the power of allowing things to be as they are?

Practice the application of this to something more personal to you in your mental health journey, like all those thoughts you have about who you should or should not be: "I won't be happy until I lose twenty pounds." "I won't be happy until I fully love myself." "I won't be happy until I feel less broken." "I should be as perfect as I can be." There are so many others. Ugh, the things we tell ourselves when no one is watching! Imagine having a different relationship with your thoughts and feelings, allowing some nonattachment, and enjoying the freedom that comes from that.

Intervention 3: Dialectical Behavioral Therapy Tools

The following exercise is directly taken from the work of Marsha Linehan, creator of dialectical behavioral therapy and an American psychologist—specifically a worksheet based on her work titled "Core Mindfulness Handout: Practicing a Nonjudgmental Stance." Linehan's focus with this skill is on practicing being more mindful of how judgments affect our emotional well-being, and if we remove the judgment, we decrease our suffering. This skill is more detailed than some of the steps related to nonattachment in the above section.

Seth Axelrod created the below worksheet based on Linehan's core mindfulness (2008).

What are judgments?

- Describing things as good or bad, valuable or worthless, smart or stupid, terrible or wonderful, beautiful or ugly, etc.
- Describing how things "should" or "shouldn't" be
- Describing by comparing or contrasting

Usefulness of judgments?

- They allow for quick descriptions by creating simple categories
- They are fast, short hand for describing preferences and consequences

Problems with judgments?

- They often distract from reality (judgments may replace facts; when we judge we often stop observing)
- They tend to feed negative emotions (anger, guilt, shame)
- Positive judgments are fragile: anything judged "good" can also be judged "bad"

Steps for letting go of judgments

1. Practice noticing judgments. Keep a count of judgments.
2. Ask yourself, "Do I want to be judging?" "Is the judging helping or hurting me?"
3. Replace judgments with:

- Statements of preference: "I like ..." "I prefer ..." or "I wish ..."
- Statements of consequences: "This is helpful/harmful for ...", "This is effective/ineffective for ..."
- Statements of fact: "This thing happened in this way, at this time ..."

4. Practice accepting what is (facts, preferences, consequences) and letting go of the judgments. Let the judgments drift away.
5. Remember not to judge your judging!

Core Mindfulness Worksheet

Practicing Nonjudgmental Stance

1. Identify a judgment about yourself, someone else, or some situation.
2. Describe your reasons for letting go of this judgment.
3. Replace the judgments with descriptions of facts, consequences, and/or your preferences about this.
4. Practice accepting the nonjudgmental descriptions and letting go of the judgments. Identify any words, actions (e.g., relaxation), body postures, or imagery that helps you let go.
5. Remember not to judge your judging!
6. Describe any changes you noticed in your acceptance or your emotions as you practiced nonjudgmental stance.

Now let's apply this to a situation in relation to caring for a loved one with mental illness by responding to the worksheet prompts.

1. **Identify a judgment about yourself, someone else, or some situation.**

    "I am being a selfish caregiver. I am not doing enough. I shouldn't be this selfish; it is bad."

2. **Describe your reasons for letting go of this judgment**

    - It's causing me distress to shame myself and making me feel like a horrible person.

    - It's judging myself for something I don't deserve to be judged for.

3. **Replace the judgments with descriptions of facts, consequences, and/or your preferences about this.**

    - A fact is that I have done several things for my mother/loved one over the past month. It's not true that "I am not doing enough." And it's just me feeling this right now in this moment because of the pressure I put on myself to "always do the right thing."

4. **Practice accepting the nonjudgmental descriptions and letting go of the judgments.**

Identify any words, actions (e.g., relaxation), body postures, or imagery that helps you let go.

- Words that help me let go are "I am human, and I can only do so much. I give myself permission to engage in self-care as needed. I allow myself this." And I can using various other affirmations.

- Images include thinking of times I have helped her recently in order to let go of that guilt and judgment.

- Body postures and relaxation include taking mindful breaths, using grounding techniques.

5. **Remember not to judge your judging!**

"I remind myself of this gracefully."

6. **Describe any changes you noticed in your acceptance or your emotions as you practiced nonjudgmental stance.**

- I notice that my body feels more regulated. I feel less anxious. I feel less guilt and shame. I realize I am not looking at this situation in a good-versus-bad nature, more that it "just is." I am noticing my stance changing and accepting my experience.

Take a moment to practice this before reading on. Run through an experience you've had recently with your loved one, and notice how your mind shifts to a more relaxed, less judgmental place.

Now, let's try this in relation to our own mental health— the apples.

1. **Identify a judgment about yourself, someone else, or some situation.**

   "I am crazy and I come from a crazy family and I am going to end up getting schizophrenia. I am doomed."

2. **Describe your reasons for letting go of this judgment**

   - It is causing me distress. It is making me believe that something is bad about me.

3. **Replace the judgments with descriptions of facts, consequences, and/or your preferences about this.**

   - A fact is that I do not display symptoms of schizophrenia. I am simply stressed from loving someone who does.

   - I cannot predict the future.

   - A consequence of holding onto this judgment is that it will take over my thoughts, and I do not want that.

4. **Practice accepting the nonjudgmental descriptions and letting go of the judgments. Identify any words, actions (e.g., relaxation), body postures, or imagery that helps you let go.**

   - I am not the same person as my loved one. I am a different individual than her with different life experiences.

   - I take some mindful breaths, use grounding techniques, and visualize myself as my own person on a separate life path.

5. **Remember not to judge your judging!**

   "I gracefully remind myself to not judge in this process."

6. **Describe any changes you noticed in your acceptance or your emotions as you practiced nonjudgmental stance.**

   I feel less attached to the idea that I will end up with the illness. My body and mind feel more at ease. I am more present in the moment and not judging my experiences.

If you identify with worrying about your own mental health, how did that exercise feel for you? Was it challenging or easier to let go of the judgment than you thought?

Another tool from dialectical behavioral therapy that I found helpful is Linehan's list of legitimate rights ("Interpersonal Effectiveness" 2022). These are helpful affirmations in moments I needed a break and needed to give myself permission for that break.

Your Legitimate Rights

1. You have a right to need things from others.
2. You have a right to put yourself first sometimes.
3. You have a right to feel and express your emotions or your pain.
4. You have a right to be the final judge of your beliefs and accept them as legitimate.
5. You have the right to your opinions and convictions.
6. You have the right to your experience—even if it's different from that of other people.
7. You have a right to protest any treatment or criticism that feels bad to you.
8. You have a right to negotiate for change.
9. You have a right to ask for help, emotional support, or anything else you need (even though you may not always get it).
10. You have a right to say no; saying no doesn't make you bad or selfish.
11. You have a right not to justify yourself to others.
12. You have a right not to take responsibility for someone else's problem.
13. You have a right to choose not to respond to a situation.

14. You have a right, sometimes, to inconvenience or disappoint others.

As you read through these, which ones spoke to you either as part of your caregiving experience or just as an individual and something you have struggled with?

Intervention 4: Narrative Therapy Tools— Externalization of the Problem

David Epston and Michael White developed narrative therapy ("Narrative Therapy" 2018). The exercise of "naming the problem" in narrative therapy helps individuals and families identify problems and begin to view them as outside of themselves. It attempts to show you that "you are not the problem; the problem is the problem." It is taking something that you are internalizing and externalizing it.

Naming Problem Stories in Narrative Practices: Externalization

1. If we were to call all of this, all of what has been occurring in your family, a name, what would we want to name it?
2. When the problem visits, how do you know it is present?
3. Do you know what it looks like? Sounds like?
4. What do you think [the problem] wants from you?

5. What plans does [the problem] have in mind for your future?
6. Mapping the effects of the problem on relationships in the family.
7. When [the problem] is present, does it have you talking differently with one another? How do you notice this?
8. Length:
   How long has [the intruder] lived in this house? When did you first notice [the problem] coming home with you?
9. Breadth:
   Does [the intruder] live in all aspects of your life? Are there some places where it lives more than others?
10. Depth:
    Does [the problem] wreak such havoc that there are times when it makes it hard to carry on?
11. Do you have a different future planned out for your family than the future [the problem] has planned? (Hedtke 2014).

As you can see, externalization is just another way of seeing the actual problem outside of yourself, or your loved one, instead of seeing you or them as the problem. These questions are just another way to do that. So for the situation between my mother and me, neither she nor I was the problem; the problem was the problem. Psychosis symptoms were the main problem. And when we separate ourselves from that, we can find peace. You are not your illness. They are not their illness.

In this chapter, we reviewed four key healing tools to help forgive and release, to practice nonattachment, to practice core mindfulness and nonjudgment, and to externalize the problem.

Moment of Reflection

1. Which tool do you feel resonated with you most?
2. Which one gave you peace while reading through it?
3. Did you find any of them useful for both your caregiving experience and personal mental health experiences?
4. If you did relate with them, how can you incorporate them into your daily or weekly life to bring yourself more peace?

7

All the Selves

In this chapter, we will be talking about all the selves: self-compassion, self-acceptance, self-love, self-worth, and self-esteem, as well as your authentic self, trusting yourself, and trusting intuition. These tools are for you to use in your caregiving journey and the journey to yourself.

Take what resonates with you, and leave what doesn't. It's a collection of things I have come across as a therapist that I personally have utilized with myself to get through the hard times. They may not resonate with you. Some of them will apply only to your own internal struggles as a person, and some will apply to general experiences of a caregiver.

Intervention 5: Self Compassion and Grace

Self-compassion is nurturing yourself
with all the kindness and love you would
shower on someone you cherish.
— Debra L. Rebble, PhD

Self-compassion is being kind and understanding
when confronted with personal feelings.
— Kristen Neff (2022)

Neff talks about three elements of self-compassion (2022). The first is refraining from judgment of the self, instead being warm and understanding toward ourselves when we fail or feel inadequate. The second is accepting that suffering and personal inadequacy are part of the shared human experience and something we all go through, rather than something that happens to "me alone." And the third element is being mindful over our emotions and thoughts and creating balance to have clarity.

So what does it mean? Simply put, treat yourself like your own best friend. Give yourself grace and understanding during trials in life and refrain from judgment of yourself. It's asking yourself, "How can I care for and comfort myself in this moment?"

Neff developed a Self-Compassion Scale to evaluate your sense of self-compassion. It poses twelve statements that you rate on a 1–5 scale (1 = almost never, 5 = almost always). For caregivers of a loved one with mental illness, it serves as a nice self-check for times you are having difficulty caring for someone with severe mental illness.

The following are the twelve statements it contains.

1. When I fail at something important to me, I become consumed by my feelings of inadequacy.
2. I try to be understanding and patient toward those aspects of my personality I don't like.
3. When something painful happens I try to take a balanced viewpoint of the situation.
4. When I'm feeling down, I tend to feel like most other people are probably happier than I am.
5. I try to see my failings as part of the human condition.
6. When I'm going through a very hard time, I give myself the caring and tenderness I need.
7. When something upsets me I try to keep my emotions in balance.
8. When I fail at something that is important to me, I tend to feel alone in my failure.
9. When I'm feeling down I tend to obsess and fixate on everything that's wrong.
10. When I feel inadequacy in some way, I try to remind myself that feelings of inadequacy are shared by most people.
11. I'm disapproving and judgmental about my own flaws and inadequacies.
12. I'm intolerant and impatient towards those aspects of my personality I don't like.

When you read over those twelve statements, what did you feel? For me, I feel like I have permission to feel whatever the heck I am feeling and that I am not alone in my pain. They also give me permission to cut myself some slack. We all need that, right? We need the ability to just have compassion with ourselves when we make errors and feel like we have to be infallible human beings.

Another aspect of this scale is that you can tailor it even further to fit your own needs. For example, you could add statements specific to your experience with self-compassion scale and rate them. I might add one such as, "When my mother's psychosis persisted today, I allowed myself to feel agitated." You can make them more specific and even turn them into affirmations.

Examples of Self-Compassion Affirmations for Caregivers

- I am human and allowed to feel all of my emotions that come up as a result of caregiving for someone with severe mental illness.
- I allow myself to acknowledge that caretaking for someone with mental illness is challenging.
- I allow myself time and space to be tender toward my emotions surrounding my loved one and the agitation I may feel.
- I won't judge myself for being angry with this situation with my loved one.
- I will give myself grace and understanding toward this situation.

- I accept myself on my worst days when I may yell at my loved one.
- I am free to let go of other people's judgments of me in my caretaking role.

What specific-to-you affirmations would you create to give yourself compassion through your caregiving experience?

> Grace is the face that love wears when it meets with imperfection. (Cooke 1975)

We all deserve to give ourselves grace, no matter what we are going through.

Intervention 6: Self-Love, Self-Acceptance, Self-Worth, Self-Esteem

We have four more *self* words to briefly cover, and they have different meanings.

Self-esteem is a feeling of confidence, satisfaction, and respect for yourself and your abilities. Self-esteem at times is measured more by external factors such as achievements to define worth.

Self-worth is the internal sense of being good enough or worthy of love and belonging from others. It's a sense of one's own value as a human being.

Self-love is an appreciation of one's own worth or virtue.

And self-acceptance is acceptance of all of one's attributes, positive or negative. When we are self-accepting, we embrace every part of ourselves and integrate all our attributes.

The point of all the *self* words (as I am starting to feel self-absorbed when writing so many *self*s) is to just be aware of how they differ for the purposes of evaluating yourself and where you feel you are in your self-acceptance journey.

These are some affirmations for self-acceptance.

- I honor my life's path.
- I am growing wiser each day.
- I accept myself for my flaws as part of the human existence.
- My mistakes are just growth opportunities.
- I accept that I will not be able to please everyone, as no one can do that.

Affirmations for self-worth include these:

- I am worthy of love.
- I am worthy of receiving patience from others.
- I am worthy of belonging.
- I am at peace with myself.
- I am a valuable human being.

Some self-love affirmations are as follow:

- I appreciate that I have worked hard to get where I am today.

- I appreciate that I value myself and make healthy choices.
- I am a good person who deserves happiness.
- I am so much stronger than I realize.
- I have the power to face any difficulty.

All this has me channeling a song right now—"Unstoppable" by Sia. "I'm so powerful, I don't need batteries today."

All of these *self* concepts tend to overlap. I just wanted to distinguish the differences in the *self* words so you could assess and see which resonates with you best, if at all. The thing about using affirmations is that you should first create ones you feel that you naturally resonate with and believe on some level. Otherwise, they can feel like "toxic positivity," meaning that we are denying negative emotions as if they do not exist or overinflating something positive, as if we need to have only a positive mindset. That is toxic positivity because it's impossible to feel positive all the time. Effective affirmations make sense to you at that time, matter to you, and have healing effects.

Likewise, remember earlier in this book when I mentioned assessing boundaries daily and how there is a need to interchange them based on the day or week? The same holds true for affirmations as a healing tool. It depends on where you are in your own journey. You may wake up one day and feel the deep need to dive into some affirmations for support and the next day say, "Nope, hell no. I need something else."

This is one of my hopes for my readers, that you understand that I am not structuring my suggestions as a step-by-step guide for you to follow to get through your journey. I am saying that you need to assess as you go based on what resonates with you at any point on your journey. What works one day may not work the next. *I am saying that using your own discernment is what matters most throughout the entire journey.* No one knows *you* better than *you*. This is also why I utilize an eclectic approach, throwing things in this book from a few different theories. There is no one-size-fits-all model.

Affirmations are not the only tool for improving the "selves." Thousands of online tools, meditations, journaling exercises, and psychology theories are available as well.

Intervention 7: Gratitude Practice

Another helpful intervention for caregivers for people with severe mental illness is practicing gratitude. Robert Emmons is a leading gratitude psychologist who says there are two parts or components to gratitude (2010). The first is that we affirm the good things we have received, and the second is that we acknowledge the roles other people play in providing our life with goodness. Gratitude practices that would help facilitate this include journaling, writing a letter, saying thank you, expressing thanks to others, and many more.

So the question is, How do we find gratitude in our lives while caring for someone with severe mental illness? You may already do one or some of these interventions. Here is a list of things I have gratitude toward as part of my journey with my mother.

- I am thankful for my friends who listened to me endlessly even if they didn't know what to say at times.
- I am grateful for understanding bosses when I needed time off from work to care for her.
- I am grateful to my family members for listening when I needed them, offering caregiving support for a couple of hours, and other things.
- I am grateful that I had a home, food, and water during those times of difficulty.
- I am grateful that, for a few days out of the week, there has not been a crisis with my loved one.
- I am grateful that, when some of the crises did occur, they weren't any worse than they were, as they could have been
- I am grateful for the Christmas cards that my mother's friends, our family, and our friends sent during her last Christmas.
- I am grateful for every text and phone call that friends and loved ones sent during difficult times and, even more, quiet times to check in.
- I am grateful that today my mother laughed and made me laugh.
- I am grateful that I had enough money to survive and get our needs met this month.
- I am grateful for the hospice team who would come and show compassion at every visit toward both her and me.
- I am thankful I had a working vehicle to drive places I needed to go.

- I am grateful for the community's help when my mother went missing.
- I am thankful for all the helpers in the social services, public service, and medical fields.

I could continue, but I want to give you a chance to think and reflect now. This idea may seem so simple or like it should be easy to maintain this mindset before, during, and after any crises or day-to-day operations of caring for a loved one. But it's not so easy. We all work and operate in our lives on such a structured routine, the days blending from one to the next, that we don't always stop to reflect. In moments when we feel so defeated, these are the moments when gratitude reflection is helpful.

And we all innately know that, in an instant, any of the above-mentioned things can be stripped away from us quickly and randomly through a job loss, a pandemic, a financial change, or the loss of another friend or family member. We all know this is how life works. Yet due to time and stress, we forget the gratitude piece. Again, we are not practicing toxic positivity here. We are examining what we are truly grateful for in our experiences and daily lives.

At the beginning of the book on the dedication page, you can see quotes from my mother's epitaph, which I read at her funeral: "The Ten Lessons I Learned from My Mom." I removed the content between the quotes, as some things are only meant for me to know. Yet this is how I showed gratitude toward her, through letter writing. If you see that to be suited for your needs, write letters.

As I mentioned earlier, use your discernment regarding if or when it makes sense or is helpful to you to use gratitude in your process.

Intervention 8: Trusting Intuition and Yourself

Learning to trust our intuition or gut feelings is another tool. If we really stop and listen to what our intuition is telling us, it often warns us of things we should or shouldn't do. It can help guide us in making decisions that are best for ourselves and loved ones in this mental health journey. Think of a time when you went against a gut feeling that you had and how that impacted you. Usually, we end up feeling regret for not listening to our guts.

Intuition is "the ability to understand something immediately, without conscious reasoning." Browne (2021) explains it as follows.

There are three types of intuition:

Coherence and Insight—Knowing something without knowing the source of that knowledge. This largely correlates with IQ.

Implicit Learning—Not knowing that you know something. This is picking up cognitive patterns.

> **Subjective Intuitive Abilities**—Thinking you know something. This is for the intellectually curious who like puzzles and philosophical debates. They tend to prefer intuitive thinking.

Kristin Galli Hankins gives six steps to trusting your intuition and yourself (2022): 1) doing mindfulness work of some kind (breathing, meditation, etc.) to quiet the mind, 2) doing a body scan to assess where you are feeling things in your body, 3) repeatedly telling yourself, *I trust myself*, 4 and 5) feeling how truth and falsehood feel on your body, and 6) noticing the difference between true and false statements you tell yourself.

Thus, the key to intuition is simply quieting the mind, getting into a regulated state of peace, and assessing where you feel things on your body. When we quiet the mind, answers regarding what feels good for us come more naturally because they are not forced.

I love these six steps because they focus on feeling the differences between false and true in the body. I know that, when I am making decisions based on what other people ask of me or when I really don't want to do something, those false statements somatically trigger my stomach. It feels heavy. I feel sensations in my head as well. I know I feel things strongly when I do not trust my intuition and say no when I really want to.

When it comes to trusting intuition as part of your healing journey, it is a powerful tool. You no longer do things that are out of alignment with who you are and your true authentic self. You can sense things before they happen at times. You stop second-guessing yourself and feeling indecisive about things and start doing things based on your truest heart's desires.

Moment of Reflection: Gratitude

1. In what form do you show gratitude to others— letters, affirmations, journaling?
2. For what do you think you could show more gratitude? What would be healing for you?

Moment of Reflection: Intuition

1. In your caregiving experience, have there been moments when your intuition told you something and you didn't listen to it, but it turned out to be right?
2. In your caregiving experience, have there been moments when your intuition told you something and you followed that gut feeling?
3. What about in matters of romance, career, friendships, or family relationships?

The upward turn, reconstruction and working through, and acceptance and hope—all of the interventions above are part of these last three stages of grief. Again, the healing process is not linear.

8

Balancing of Energy

Earlier in this book, we talked about the need for self-regulation through any of our crises or experiences of caregiving in mental health. This chapter will briefly explain the science behind our nervous system and the fight, flight, or freeze response. It will also explore the seven-chakra energy system, the concept of HeartMath, the feminine and masculine energy in all of us, the energy of various emotions, the energy of fear and ego, and how to consider all of this when balancing inner harmony.

We will then take time to apply this knowledge to our experiences of caregiving and how to regulate more specifically based on our needs and our bodies' somatic responses to stress.

The Autonomic Nervous System

The autonomic nervous system (ANS) is a part of the nervous system that regulates most of the body's internal functions. Two systems within the ANS interact to maintain cardiovascular activity in its optimal range and to permit appropriate reactions to changing external and internal conditions. These are the sympathetic nervous system and the parasympathetic nervous system (Lanese and Dutfield 2022).

The sympathetic nervous system is our "alarm system," or the fight-or-flight side to the system. It works to alert us to danger or threatening situations. The nerves within this system accelerate our heart rate and cause other somatic symptoms of stress.

The parasympathetic nervous system works to "rest and digest," or to slow our bodies' responses down. It tries to counter our fight-or-flight response.

If these two systems are out of balance, the consequences can be long-term physical health issues. However, this isn't a science lesson. I just wanted to give quick definitions relevant to what we are discussing.

The Fight, Flight, Freeze, or Fawn Response

The fight-or-flight response is based in the sympathetic nervous system. The amygdala is the part of the brain that is responsible for fear. It responds to fear by transmitting signals to the hypothalamus, stimulating the ANS. The underlying goal of our sympathetic nervous system is to escape something that we interpret as unsafe so that, ultimately, we can return to a state of calm and control (Frothingham 2021).

Walter Cannon developed the fight, flight, freeze, or fawn model of the system (Lavoie 2022). We fight when we aggressively react to a perceived threat. Flight involves running away from danger or perceived danger. We freeze when we are unable to move or act against a threat, and we Fawn when we immediately act to try and please someone to avoid conflict.

When we are in fight mode, we may feel the following: intense anger, urge to physically hurt someone, urge to verbally argue, crying, and somatic symptoms such as an upset stomach or bodily tightness.

When we are in the flight mode, we may feel the following; restlessness in the body, urge to run away from something, fidgety, tense or trapped, and some additional somatic symptoms such as numbness or dilated eyes.

When we are in freeze mode, we do just that—we freeze and do nothing (neither fight nor flight). Somatically, we may feel our heart rates accelerating or feel stiff as if we can't move, numbness, a sense of dread, or stuck.

When we are in fawn mode, we may feel the need to avoid a fight, flight, or freeze response and instead do whatever we can to avoid conflict altogether. Instead, we want to just please others. Fawning occurs mostly in people who grew up in abusive families. It's the desire to be overly agreeable to keep things calm.

While caregiving for my loved one with a severe mental illness, I engaged in all four of these responses at different times in regard to how I dealt with my mother's specific psychosis symptoms.

- Fight: I once threw a water bottle in my kitchen out of anger and rage about her symptoms. I felt the desire to punch things. I also argued with my mother about her symptoms at various times in our journey.
- Flight: I would walk away from or leave my mother at times when her symptoms became too much. I felt my heart rate increasing rapidly.
- Freeze: Earlier in this book, I gave an example of talking to my mother on my deck about my life, and her symptoms spiked to the point that I could not talk to her. I froze in that situation. I didn't feel I could fight or fly from that situation, so I sat in numbness.
- Fawn: Countless times, I did not argue with my mother about her symptoms. I caved in and did things for her to keep the peace, such as helping with laundry, groceries, and so on. I feel the fawning response is very easily relatable when it comes to helping those with severe mental illness. There are many times we feel we have to fawn to keep them safe. At times, I felt that, if

I did not fawn or give in to help, her symptoms would worsen. So essentially, I fawned to keep her symptoms more balanced and at peace, thinking, *If I just help her out with groceries, she will have some peace and her voices won't be as crazy today, and thus, I can also have more peace.*

I want to make sure I really clarify the definitions or symptoms of fawning, as I do not want to make it seem that, every time you "cave in" or help your loved one, you are fawning. That is not the message. As we talked about earlier regarding our values of wanting to be good children, spouses, or other loved ones for our own loved one with illness, there is a difference between wanting to help because of our values and the fawning response. Fawning is wanting to say no but not doing so, repeatedly or chronically. And generally, when we are caretaking for a physically sick loved one, we want to say no sometimes but choose not to because helping aligns with our values and because we want to help even if we are tired.

Fawning is more of a "perpetual inability to say 'no' even when a request inconveniences you" (Sengwe 2021). It is repressing your own needs for the sake of making everyone around you happy, feeling responsible for the reactions of others, having a difficult time standing up for yourself, having constant feelings of guilt, constantly looking to others to see how you are supposed to feel about a situation or relationship, or feeling as though you don't have your own identity.

Thus, fawning is not just the inability to say no during a specific life event. It is a response that you see across your life domains and relationships. If you are likely to engage in fawning during your caregiving experience, you are likely to engage in fawning in your work life, friendships, and romantic relationships as well. If you are only engaging in fawning as part of your caregiving experience, then that is more situational. Fawning is an attempt to avoid abuse.

So to specify further, the reason I engaged in fawning during interactions with my mother is that I did the same thing while growing up with her as well, even prior to knowing about her diagnosis. I engaged in fawning across all my life domains and settings.

If I told my mother no in response to her request that I help her with laundry that day or give her money for food, my mother would respond with reactions that felt like conditional love, like "You are cruel for not helping me," or "I don't want to talk to you anymore." She would hang up on me if we were on the phone, ignore my subsequent phone calls, and otherwise give me the cold shoulder. She would stop talking to me for a week if I said no to something.

So, to keep the peace, I would do things I did not want to do. I knew that, if I just sucked it up and did those things, there would be less chaos and she would be safe. Furthermore, if I lost contact with her, I feared that she would be dead in a ditch somewhere without my knowing. That is a pretty big fear and reason to keep fawning occasionally. I am not saying I didn't say no and stick to it at times, yet overall—I would say 65 to 70 percent of the time over the eight years I cared for her—I said yes. Bigger consequences would have occurred if I had said no to her more often.

Another huge consequence to saying no to my mother in regard to any financial requests was that her psychosis would start pulling me into her delusions and hallucinations. She would say things such as, "You are in on it with them," "You got money from them and aren't helping me!" or "I know you got that settlement money! They told me, and you are lying!" In response, I would start fighting: "No, Mom, I am not in on anything and have no idea what you are talking about."

When that didn't work, I felt fawning was the best choice. If I became part of her hallucinations and delusions, she would not let me in to help her; she would isolate herself from me. And I was the only one in her life at this time who had any relationship with her. So if I hadn't helped her, she would have had no one. And as I write this, I cry. What a horrible dynamic for any of us to be in—to have that sense of obligation and duty to put up with psychosis symptoms. It is a sense of having absolutely no freedom or autonomy in these decisions because, if I make the wrong choice, there is a lot at stake. Lose my mother completely? No, thank you. I will fawn.

So many people would say, "You are enabling her." I want to make it clear that I was not enabling her as much as trying to keep her alive and safe. Our system did not allow for me to *not* fawn—that is my point. I had to do things that operated like enabling because of the nature of psychosis itself. Correction: I didn't have to. But again, what would the consequences have been had I not given in and given her things she needed to live, to just survive?

Our system can't help people who don't want the help or who don't think they are sick. So who is left to help them? Us, the family members, the close friends, the people on the outskirts. We are left to our own devices to try and discern where the line between enabling and helping is. Change the system, and that line changes.

One example of the line in the system is this. Had the Area on Aging been able to continue providing services without my mother's consent, they could have given her the financial resources she needed for her food, bills, and more. But because the rules say that people need to consent to service to receive service, they discontinued services and closed her case.

If that standard of needing consent for resource-based services did not exist, how much of the world's problems in regard to mental health could be fixed? I wouldn't have had to give her my money; she could have had her own to sustain a living. Thus, wouldn't even the homelessness level decrease?

Couldn't a new standard of care for resource-based services reduce the need for that consenting signature and just drop off the darn food? Drop off the vouchers for food? Give it to the family, loved ones, or guardians to manage for the people with mental illness? Why is everything so complicated in a system that is meant to be helpful? With one easy change, these issues would dissipate.

How can we change our fawning behaviors when it comes to caretaking for a loved one with mental illness? We go back to boundaries to. As I said earlier in the book in regard to boundaries, there is no one-size-fits-all model.

These are all expected responses to stressful situations. So what tool can we use to get through these moments? It is self-regulation, the ability to regulate our nervous systems in the moment. Self-regulation does not mean our feelings are invalid. It helps us to manage our somatic symptoms of stress to keep our bodies in a state of homeostasis so we can get through it.

Examples of self-regulation include breath work, grounding techniques, meditation, muscle-relaxation exercises, being out in nature, journaling, and visualization. All of these techniques and more assist us in regulating our ANS. So the tool is being aware of how our nervous systems are impacted and practicing some of these skills to utilize during times of crisis with our loved ones.

Fawning: Ways to Unlearn It

Dylan Finch writes about ways to unlearn the fawn response of trauma (2020). He suggests asking yourself the following questions during a conflict.

1. Does the stance I am taking and my reaction to this person feel aligned with my values?
2. Am I deeply respecting humanity of the person in front of me (while being seen and held in my humanity)?
3. Am I speaking from the heart?
4. Am I being authentic—or am I giving apologies that I don't mean or appeasing somebody else for the sake of it?
5. Am I taking responsibility for how I'm showing up while not burdening myself with what isn't mine to hold?
6. Am I looking to quickly exit this conversation to avoid discomfort, or move toward a common ground that supports us both, even if I have to endure some discomfort along the way?

In short, am I coming from a place of self-honor or self-betrayal?

For me, I relate to the second question in regard to caregiving for a person with mental illness. It was always about respecting my mother's humanity and her needs.

Finch further recommends sitting with the anger and disappointment of others, getting in touch with your personal values, giving yourself permission to feel and name your feelings, and paying attention to how others communicate their needs to you.

The Seven-Chakra Energy System

The seven chakras in the human body were mentioned in spiritual texts as early as 1500–1000 BC (Stelter 2016). They are not a new concept by any means. Yet, in traditional therapy, they are not widely utilized. Many healers, yogis, and spiritual teachers in today's society utilize knowledge of the seven chakras for healing, spiritual advancement, and holistic approaches.

I mention them here as they are another tool for healing on your mental health journey, whether you are caring for a loved one with mental illness or caring for yourself. There is value in balancing the chakra system to feel balanced in your everyday life and to have more peace, harmony, and awareness in your caregiving experience.

Chakra means "wheel" and refers to energy points or spiritual power points in your body. There are seven main chakras along your spine, starting at the tailbone area and finishing at your head. Some people believe there are up to 114 chakras total in the human body.

The Main Seven Chakras

1. The Root Chakra: This is located at the base of your spine, in the tailbone area. The color associated with it is red. It is responsible for physical identity, stability, and grounding.
2. The Sacral Chakra: This is located just above the pubic bone but below the belly button. The

color associated with it is orange. Its meaning is sexuality, pleasure, and creativity.

3. The Solar Plexus Chakra: This is located in the upper abdomen in the stomach area. The color associated with it is yellow. Its meaning is self-esteem and confidence.

4. The Heart Chakra: This is located in the center of the chest just above the heart, the area called "the heart center" by yogian friends. The color associated with it is green. Its meaning is love and compassion.

5. The Throat Chakra: This is located in the throat. The color associated with it is blue. Its meaning is communication.

6. The Third Eye Chakra: This is located between the eyes on your forehead. It is also called the "brow chakra." The color associated with it is indigo (shade of purple). Its meaning is intuition and imagination.

7. The Crown Chakra: This is located on the top of your head. The colors associated with it are white or violet. Its meaning is awareness or intelligence. (Stelter 2016)

The idea behind the chakras is that, if one is "blocked," it can cause emotional distress or imbalance. If your throat chakra is blocked, it can cause you to not speak your truth in verbal conversations, which causes distress. If there is a block in the sacral chakra, it can lower your feelings of confidence, self-worth, or sexual pleasure and drive.

Blocked chakras can also cause physical issues where the chakras are located. For example, if there is a blockage in your third-eye chakra, you may experience headaches or concentration problems. If there is a blockage in your heart chakra, it can manifest in heart problems, asthma, or weight issues.

I am very new to learning about and understanding the chakras. I didn't have any true interest in them until this year, when my awakening began. I previously believed and respected that they existed, yet I didn't see the practical usefulness of them. Thus, I understand if it is hard for you to buy into this concept and utilize chakras for your own balancing of energy and healing. I started to buy into the modality once I started meditating and noticed physical pain dissipate in certain areas of my body.

I will say that I have personally felt physical results of my awakening and from using guided mediations that unblock my chakras. For example, for the past couple of years, I have had lower back pain because I have a broken tailbone, and I have received chiropractic care for years. The pain never fully subsided. I would go for my adjustment, and nothing would feel different afterward for any length of time. Once I started doing guided mediations, I felt that pain subside. I also do yoga occasionally.

The root chakra is the one closest to the tailbone. The time of my life when I felt the most pain is when I did not have stability in my life at all—not enough finances, not feeling grounded and present, and not feeling like my basic needs were met. Once I started doing the meditations and some light yoga, I felt a release of pain in that area like no other. I also started to balance out all seven chakras through those meditations, and my whole body felt less pain. I have continued doing both inner and outer self work to accomplish that.

There is a great guided mediation for clearing your seven chakras on YouTube by Magnetize Yourself (2021). It's about twenty minutes long. The developer goes through each of the seven chakras, providing affirmations for each. It helps you identify where you are blocked, what you are feeling, and what you need. I have done this one several times and continue to do it at least once per week. Each week, I notice something slightly different. I also sometimes see the color of the corresponding chakra during mediations, depending on which chakra is blocked.

One week I felt, or noticed, that, when the speaker was giving the affirmations for the throat chakra, I felt angry. I started to have this awareness of a specific situation with a friend that I was angry about, which just indicated I wasn't communicating well with this person and that it was affecting me more than I realized. Had I not done that meditation, it may have taken longer for me to become aware that something was even bothering me at the time. That is the thing about meditations: you can do the same guided meditation on multiple occasions and experience something different each time. But the awareness of it is very helpful.

I didn't use the concepts of chakras or meditation when I was personally going through my caregiving experience, and I truly wonder what that would have been like had I used them. While thinking of the relational trauma of interactions with my mother, I wonder what would have come up during that clearing. I imagine I would have felt blockages in every one of the seven chakras, and at various degrees and intensities across different weeks. And had I used this as a tool, could I have balanced myself better, engaged in self-care differently, and interacted with her differently?

Would it be beneficial for you to buy into these ideas (if you haven't already)? It would most definitely bring you new awareness that could support you on your journey. It would also give you new ideas on how to handle situations to meet your needs.

You saw a lot of these points earlier in my mother's story. You probably even felt physical sensations while reading her story that were brought up for you and your chakras because of relatable points in your story. Maybe you felt a throat chakra blockage when reading about the difficulties in the mental health system? Something to think about.

The balancing of the chakras can be a powerful healing tool. It's constantly there for you, as energy is always changing. The nature of life and experiences of mental health and caregiving are transient.

This leads to the concept of the HeartMath program and the idea of heart coherence.

HeartMath and Heart Coherence

One day I decided to turn on the Gaia Network to try and learn something new on my spiritual journey. I came across a short series about HeartMath and consciousness. And then I realized it was this whole amazing program and certification process.

HeartMath Institute has studied for twenty-five years the psychophysiology of stress, emotions, and the interactions between the heart and brain ("The Science of HeartMath" 2021). Their research found that the heart communicates with the brain more so than the brain communicates with the heart. They talk about how previous knowledge placed most emphasis on the brain's being the primary communicator to the heart and ordering it through neural signals. But they found that the communication between them is a two-way street, as they are constantly responding to each other.

This is why HeartMath believes that the idea of heart coherence is essential in stress management and sustainable behavior change. "Coherence is the state when the heart, mind, and emotions are in energetic alignment and cooperation," HeartMath Institute Research Director Dr. Rollin McCraty says. "It is a state that builds resiliency—personal energy is accumulated, not wasted—leaving more energy to manifest intentions and harmonious outcomes" ("The Science of HeartMath" 2021).

HeartMath defines resiliency in four domains: physical, emotional, mental, and spiritual.

Physical resilience is basically reflected in physical flexibility, endurance and strength, while emotional resilience is reflected in the ability to self-regulate, degree of emotional flexibility, positive outlook and supportive relationships. Mental resilience is reflected in the ability to sustain focus and attention, mental flexibility and the capacity for integrating multiple points of view. Spiritual resilience is typically associated with commitment to core values, intuition and tolerance of others' values and beliefs.... "We are coming to understand health not as the absence of disease, but rather as the process by which individuals maintain their sense of coherence (i.e. sense that life is comprehensible, manageable, and meaningful) and ability to function in the face of changes in themselves and their relationships with their environment."

Their research shows that the HeartMath self-regulation techniques help replace depleting emotional undercurrents with more positive, regenerative attitudes, feelings, and perceptions.

The idea of this research and program is heart coherence. If we have it, we function more optimally in the face of adversity or changes as they arise. It's understanding that, regardless of what we are going through, we can manage it in a heart-centered, compassionate manner. Such interesting research! But what a nice reminder that we are the makers of our own ability to manage and self-regulate through the heart-brain connection. Imagine how using this program could change your caregiving experience.

Balancing of Feminine and Masculine Energies

Hold on; don't roll your eyes. I know that, for some people, it may be tempting to skip this section. But don't. Read it and consider it. The theory of balancing feminine and masculine energies dates back to the beginning of time.

The theory behind this is that all humans have both masculine and feminine energies within them. It is the yin and yang of our souls, the balance of both sides of our energy that helps us through this thing called life.

Masculine Energy:

The masculine in us all is action based, logical, and assertive; provides structure; and provides confidence for ourselves and the ability to speak up for ourselves. The masculine in us all helps us in situations where we need to know or draw the line between what's wrong and what is right for us. The masculine represents strength, adventure, making changes, following through with what's on our minds, critical thinking, and survival (Salow 2011).

Feminine Energy:

The feminine in us all is more passive, willing to compromise, reflective, internal, nurturing, peaceful, harmonious, sensual, and abundant. Yet the feminine is also wild and untamed at times. The feminine paves her own way and ignores unwritten rules that society has constructed. The feminine understands the sacredness of life and trusts that her needs will be met (Salow 2011).

The theory is that there is not always an equal balance of both masculine and feminine energies within a person. At times, it's necessary for the masculine to lead in order to get things accomplished. Other times, it is necessary for the feminine to lead in order to be reflective or more nurturing. The idea is that it is more about utilizing your energies the way you need them, at the time you need them.

Now stop for a minute. Pause. For some men who identify as cisgender and heterosexual, this can be a very difficult concept to buy into. Our culture has been discussing toxic masculinity quite a bit over the past few years. "Toxic masculinity is the adherence to the limiting and potentially dangerous societal standards set for men and masculine identifying people" (White 2021). If you are a cisgender and heterosexual male who falls into this category, I am inviting you to consider embracing your inner feminine energy.

Toxic masculinity teaches men in our society that they cannot express their emotions and that, if they do, they are weak. It can cause aggression, hate, division, heterosexism, or discrimination. These men come into the therapy office because they are experiencing anger, rage, impulsivity, or emotional crying spells and cannot identify why they are feeling the way they are. Once they come into therapy and feel it is a safe space to let it all out, they cry and heal. Toxic femininity also exists.

Thus, if you are a heterosexual male, this may be something you experience. And it may be difficult for you to admit that you have feminine energy within you. But you do, and that is okay. It is also okay to admit that you want to talk to someone about your feelings, that you need that. We all do. And you have that nurturing side of the feminine, the ability to be reflective about your emotions and process them.

Now, let's apply this to your caregiving experience for a minute. During mine, there were moments when my masculine energy needed to lead, solve problems, and use critical thinking. I didn't have time to let my feminine side lead and spend too much time in reflection and analytical thinking. I had to act in moments of crisis. Can you relate with this?

My feminine side led more when it was time for physical caretaking, such as rubbing her back, bathing her, brushing her hair, being nurturing. My feminine led when I needed to be softer with myself, gentler. In moments when I had self-doubt in my role of caregiver, my feminine energy is what reminded me I was doing a good job.

There are many books, articles, and blogs on how to awaken both the feminine and masculine energies inside of you. Yet I am not here to go into that level of detail. You simply are aware that they exist and that they are both useful.

Ego Death and Authenticity

Ego comes into play here also. When we lead with too much pride or arrogance in anything, we suffer. When we want something, do something, or act as something to get something, we are acting in ego, not in love. And through spiritual awakenings, there is the concept of ego death.

Ego death refers to the process of the ego changing for enlightenment. "Ego death is the realization that you are not truly the things you identified with and that the ego, or sense of self that you created in your mind, is just a fabrication" (Regan 2022). It refers to the act of letting go of all the things we are not so we can exist in love and the true spirit of who we are.

For example, in my ego-death process, I previously believed that I couldn't write a book about spirituality and how the angels talk to me because people will think I have psychosis. Before I could write this book, I had to let go of the belief and the fears associated with this thought and realize what or who was at the core of my spirit. I had to stop being afraid of my own light, or what other people would think about my light, and realize that none of what people think or what their projections are matter.

I had to meditate to see my higher self. And once I did, I realized how beautiful of a soul she is. As are you. When I let her lead, I feel grounded, authentic, real, peaceful, and humble. When I let my ego lead, I feel full of self-doubt and negative thinking patterns. I was fearful of my own ego. If I show good parts of myself to others, they will think I am arrogant. However, when I merge and act on my higher self, the ego subsides because I feel I am acting in compassion and in my authentic self.

People project aspects of themselves onto you when you make them feel uncomfortable in some way because of issues they have within themselves. It is okay that we cannot always walk in compassion with ourselves and others. It is okay that you may experience sacred rage energy in the caregiving of a loved one, wanting to scream at the highest pitch you can to release it. It's okay to feel all of these feelings and to struggle with compassion at times. The key is to be aware that that is what is happening and to then be able to harness it, to reel it back into balance. So whether you are going through a caregiving experience or other challenging situation in your life, you have all the skills to do it well.

How do you do that?

1. Recognize that it's happening.
2. Allow yourself to feel it; sit in it and scream in it.
3. Recenter and regulate again.
4. Take that awareness and knowledge from the situation to the next situation or moment in your life.
5. Tell yourself, *I refuse to judge myself at any age or situation on my life timeline.* Repeat that several times, and be specific: *My twenty-year-old self who hurt someone I loved—I forgive and do not judge myself. My thirty-nine-year-old self who just learned the lessons I did—I forgive myself for.*

I used to want to get a tattoo of a flower with the last names of all the families I have in the petals. I have four families myself, plus two families of which I was part during earlier romantic relationships. I believe each family taught me lessons of love, of course, but all the different variations of love in families.

Every family has a pattern. Every family has problems. It's just humanity. It doesn't mean they are broken. The patterns are based on all the goals of the individuals within the family. We all carry things within us that filter into our family dynamics.

My throat chakra was blocked for a very long time. My intuition sensed intensity of emotions in my family. I can feel other people's emotions because I am an empath. It isn't a curse; it is a gift. My soul's purpose here on

Earth is to have the exact experiences I have had on the timeline that I did. Your experiences are the same, on your timeline, and you have experienced them in the time, way, and manner in which you have.

We don't have to know everything, be everything, or perfect anything at all in this world. None of us. We all put so many expectations on ourselves based on what society thinks we should be. We take all that in, it sits inside of our souls, and it darkens them. *And when we balance out that dark and light, we find harmony and inner peace.* Don't let society's current norms constrain you, define you, or contain you!

I was so afraid of my own power that I sat in darkness. In fact, I resented the word *power*. To me, it represented things that are bad, like politics or a person with egotistical characteristics. And now my understanding and relationship with the word *power* is more balanced, understood, and in congruence within myself.

When I started balancing my energies, my heart's purest intent for this book was to rally up souls going through mental health journeys with loved ones and themselves. I have envisioned going door to door to people's homes, rallying people who have gone through similar experiences, and running off together into the sunset singing *kumbaya*, with rainbows and butterflies and all things nature surrounding us as we all give one another hugs and heal together.

I am making fun of myself for a moment here. I am just a woman living in Western Pennsylvania, working as a struggling therapist. I wish I could do what I just described. That doesn't make this a delusion of grandeur because I know I don't have that power. It's just my heart's desire. It's just what I feel on a soul level every day.

Balancing Energy and Relationships

When we are in nonjudgment toward everything, our souls have so much freedom and sovereignty.

Let's say, for example, that you don't agree with the LGBTQIA community. The anger or aggression, you perceive towards their lifestyle makes you uncomfortable. By having judgments about it all, you are actually causing yourself distress that's not needed. If it bothers you, there is something inside of you that needs to be reflected upon. That does not mean your feelings about the topic are not valid and real. The feelings are very real.

For example, a father talks in therapy about his son who has disclosed that he identifies as gay. The father's feelings of confusion, sadness, grief, and worry are all valid. That father worries for his son's life. Will he be okay? Will society destroy him mentally? Will he ever find love? Will it affect his career? Plus ten other worries and thoughts. They are all valid. It's all equally as valid as the son's wanting to be accepted and loved by his father.

Another person is not directly impacted by LGBTQIA community because she doesn't have a loved one who identifies as such, but she is bothered by them just the same. So I gently ask how their identities affect her life and what she is fearful of. She has a right to the sovereignty of her own beliefs, feelings, and values surrounding the issue, yet the problem at hand is that, by having judgments, she causes herself distress. Does she realize that judgment of any kind puts her in a lower state of energy? Can she look at the souls of the people in the LGBTQIA community and see them for who they are instead of what gender or sexual identity they express? All they are longing for is acceptance of their souls.

Apply this idea of nonjudgment to any other big topic getting attention in our culture and world today. Give yourself permission to do that now. Pick a topic or belief about which you feel strongly at this moment in time— politics, LGBTQIA rights, women's rights to their bodies, financial things, psychosis, mental health, whatever. When you are in a state of thinking about this topic, sit back and examine the level of energy you are at with it. (See the energy visual.) Ask, *Can I see that it is causing me distress? Can I see that it's causing the people I love distress?* It is causing us all distress—as one, as humans.

I learned an interesting saying in therapy: "Family members often have the same mission as others. They all want the same things—to feel, to be loved and accepted by each other, to get along. It's the methods with which we choose to go about doing those that are different and misaligned." All family therapy is is an effort to align family members to realize that they have the same exact mission and to realign their ways and methods of trying to get there.

A more practical and up-to-date example is how the pandemic is breaking up families. At least once in therapists' workdays right now, a client comes into our offices in distress over a family conflict regarding the pandemic or vaccines—the classic issue is that one side of the family is not vaccinated and the other is. Think about it: it's breaking up families whose members have the same missions—to see one another, spend time together, and love one another. Their methods of getting there are just different.

We have this belief that we need to change people's beliefs in order to be happy. We can't, and we don't have the power to change others' beliefs. The idea that you need to believe what I believe in order for us to get along, like each other, and be together is so far from the truth. We absolutely do not. We just have to learn to regulate ourselves through those differences. We want to aim for you to feel safe in your beliefs without my attacking you, and vice versa. It's about offering a safe space to do that. It's compromising.

So when it comes to vaccines, as an example, we can't make people get the vaccine or not. Perhaps the end result is, "Okay, since we cannot compromise on being with each other because of our beliefs surrounding the vaccine, we change the approach. Let's just keep communicating virtually for now since that's what makes us all feel safe at this time." Remember, too, that this is just a moment in time. In one year or five years, we all may shift in our belief systems with regard to vaccines anyway. So is it really worth the battle now? Is it worth hurting one another, judging one another, and wrecking family relationships? No, absolutely not.

Take a step back and regulate. Think of yourself and how your belief system surrounding COVID has changed since March 2020 to the present date. Each individual has had their own evolution of beliefs. You have had own relationship with COVID, your own path through it. See that things do change over time. I bet that you have a unique story related to this or politics. Shifting is occurring all around us constantly. Don't fight that. Accept it, and you will feel less distress in the process.

I used COVID as the example of how energy depletion and energy imbalance affect us as individuals and in our relationships because it's likely that everyone can relate to it. However, the same idea can be applied to anything in life on which you are expending energy. Our relationships with things, concepts, ideas, and feelings change over time. Think of your twenty-year-old self versus your forty-year-old self and how much has changed for you in that span of time, including your relationships with things, concepts, ideas, and feelings. It's a revolving door of constant changes. Thus, your relationship with COVID right now may be X, but in five years it could be Y.

I am not saying to hold back your convictions, your passions in life, or things that set your soul on fire. You can still have those passions; just allow others to do the same. Be okay with that. Appreciate the compassion or passion that the other person has about what they have it about while simultaneously appreciating yours. What a magical world we would be in if we could all do that. We'd all feel emotional safety that would infuse into all domains of our lives—work, romance, friendships, family, politics, and beyond.

However, let's get back to the application of this idea of managing energies within yourself during the caregiving experience of a person with mental illness, and for yourself in general. A family sitting in one room with one individual suffering from severe mental illness needs only compassion and the ability to regulate specific to where they are at that time. The nature of that is unique across individuals and where they are with their symptoms. Meeting them where they are is always the rule in therapy.

Where, when, and what does it look like for the family members when they collectively get dysregulated? Is it the time in treatment beyond any logic of the person with severe mental illness? If so, the answer is 1) treating the ambiguous loss the caregiver is experiencing, 2) teaching all parties how to regulate as individuals, C) teaching the person with mental illness how to regulate through symptoms, and D) working with all parties to tell the others, "You are safe here. We are safe here. How can we keep making each other feel safe? When you talk about your voices or experiences, I promise to listen, to hold space for you, and vice versa."

Thus, everything and anything are all about managing energies within ourselves and within our relationships. We understand that, to do that, we must be aware of how our own energy shifts over time and how our own belief systems shift over time. In addition, feelings are not facts. Feelings are valid and real, yet that doesn't make them factual. There is no wrong or right, either, since everyone's feelings are valid. We stay in higher-level energies when we accept that.

Emotions as Energy

Esther and Jerry Hicks developed an Emotional Guidance Scale (2004). Their theory is that emotions create a vibration and that there are lower vibrational emotions and higher vibrational emotions. Esther Hicks labels twenty-two primary emotions, the lowest vibrational of which are fear, grief, desperation, despair, and powerlessness. The highest vibrational emotions are joy, appreciation, empowerment, freedom, and love.

In between the high and low point on her ladder are other emotions such as hatred, jealousy, and pessimism as well as more positive vibrational emotions such as hopefulness, enthusiasm, and optimism. Hicks states that you cannot simply jump up the ladder quickly from a lower vibrational emotion such as fear all the way to love.

Instead, you must identify where you are, move gradually, and give yourself grace.

Hicks also recommends energy work, meditation, yoga, prayer, and gratitude practice as forms to raise the vibrational energy of your emotional experience. I am referencing her work as another resource for becoming aware of your emotions and energy levels to manage your feelings in your caregiving and individual healing experience. The importance of knowledge or awareness of her work is to recognize that emotions carry vibrational energy.

Addressing Barriers to Time

At this point in the book, you may be thinking, *How the hell am I going to have time for any of this? I am a caregiver of a person with mental illness.* Or *I am a full-time worker, mother, and spouse.* I know the "I don't have time" excuse well. Let me reframe this for you. It takes only fifteen to twenty minutes per day to get in the base amount of self-care. Some days you need more than that.

The tools for mindfulness, nonjudgments, affirmations of the self, or any of the thinking and balancing regulation activities or exercises take only twenty minutes tops. The key is determining how much self-care you personally need at a baseline level.

For myself, for example, I know I require a lot as I am an empath. I need one to two hours per day of self-care to stay balanced. My one to two hours typically consist of exercising, journaling, reading, and meditating. However, this is now, after my mother has passed, and I am able to sustain this at this time of my life. During my caregiving years, I could find only fifteen to sixty minutes per day at best. I recognize that for you.

I want to go back to the idea that healing is not linear or time oriented. We can't heal by a certain date. It's the small changes we make daily that win the race in pretty much everything we do. Slowly shifting your mind into other ways of thinking will lessen distress over time and stay balanced.

Try this out for thirty days. See where the barriers are to making your self-care practice or your healing journey be what you want. Track your ratings and feelings daily and see how they change over time by the thirtieth day. Did your energy shift from drained, depleted, and negative to neutral, positive, and balanced?

You can find a daily self-monitoring chart at the end of the book in Appendix B to assess your needs for self-care.

Conclusion

The human body is an energy system. Our emotions, thoughts, feelings, and spirituality are all related. Life is a constant balancing of all of them, as we all know. Yet achieving this balance is particularly difficult when we are caregiving. You have the permission, power, and ability at any time to stop and take a few moments for yourself, even if you have children around. Regulate together. You deserve it.

Moment of Reflection: Fight, Flight, Freeze, Fawn

1. Have you experienced all four of these responses at various times of your life?
2. Have you experienced all four of these responses while caregiving for your loved one with mental illness?
3. Thinking about the responses you have experienced, what did you notice about your symptoms? Did you have strong physical or somatic symptoms that you recall?
4. If you have engaged in a fawning response before, take a moment to acknowledge that. It is not as widely known as the first three responses discussed. In what ways have you fawned to keep the peace?
5. Can you think of other areas of your life in which you have engaged in fawning?

Moment of Reflection: The Chakras

1. In what areas of your body do you physically feel your stress?
2. To what chakras do you currently relate? Are there any you feel are blocked or needing some awareness?

3. In your caregiving experience, can you think of times when your throat chakra was blocked and thus you didn't communicate something you wanted to?

4. In your caregiving experience, can you think of times when your solar plexus chakra was blocked and you could not gain confidence regarding making decisions for your loved one's care?

5. In your caregiving experience, can you think of times when your heart chakra was blocked and the love and compassion felt absent or blocked?

6. What about the sacral chakra and feelings around self-worth in your caregiving experience?

Moment of Reflection: Feminine and Masculine Energies

1. In what ways have you felt both the feminine and masculine energies in your caretaking experience? At what intensity did you feel those?

2. In what ways could you use your feminine energy more often to nurture yourself more?

3. In what ways could you utilize your masculine energy more to plan, think logically, or think critically?

4. If you are not in a caretaking experience, what about other areas of your life—work, school, friendships or family relationships, and other challenging life situations?

5. Would you consider using this theory in your everyday life to help balance out all of your experiences?

Moment of Reflection: Ego and Authenticity

1. What is your heart's desire?
2. How do you already step into your power, your authentic self? In what ways do you want to step into that more?
3. How can you let your light shine more without fear?

Moment of Reflection: Balancing Energy and Relationships

1. At what moments in your life could you balance out your own energy for the sake of your relationships?
2. Do you agree or disagree that most difficult things in relationships can be worked through by allowing each other emotional safety in conversations?
3. If you do agree, can you see your own role within some dynamics in your life in which you did or did not provide emotional safety in conversation for someone?

PART THREE

Healing Models for the Future

Cleaning up the avalanches and making
the apples taste all the sweeter.

In the first part of this book, we discussed what it's like watching someone you love suffer with mental illness in the current system of care. In the second part, we discussed what it feels like to be a family member struggling with your own mental health and tools for healing.

In this third section, we will explore how to put it all together for future models of care. We will explore generational trauma and ways to break cycles in family lines, how to talk to adolescents about mental health, regulation steps for individuals and families in treatment, and alternative and holistic models of care for the future of mental health treatment.

9

Generational Trauma

Repeat after me: "I am not my trauma. My trauma is a part of me. While my trauma is not my fault, I actively take part in healing it for myself and future generations. My trauma is what shaped me into this magnificent human— this human who is wanting, yearning, driving for change. I am powerful beyond measure, capable, compassionate, and loving. We can work together to heal each other."

We are the generation capable of making these changes because we believe in personal growth and development. We believe in the power of various therapy and healing modalities that generations before us in our culture generally did not.

Generational Trauma Defined

The *American Psychological Association Dictionary* says that intergenerational trauma is

> a phenomenon in which the descendants of a person who has experienced a terrifying event show adverse emotional and behavioral reactions to the event that are similar to those of the person himself or herself. These reactions vary by generation but often include shame, increased anxiety and guilt, a heightened sense of vulnerability and helplessness, low self-esteem, depression, suicidality, substance abuse, dissociation, hypervigilance, intrusive thoughts, difficulty with relationships and attachment to others, difficulty in regulating aggression, and extreme reactivity to stress. The exact mechanisms of the phenomenon remain unknown but are believed to involve effects on relationship skills, personal behavior, and attitudes and beliefs that affect subsequent generations. The role of parental communication about the event and the nature of family functioning appear to be particularly important in trauma transmission. Research on intergenerational trauma concentrated initially on the children, grandchildren,

and great-grandchildren of survivors of
the Holocaust and Japanese American
internment camps, but it has now
broadened to include American Indian
tribes, the families of Vietnam War
veterans, and others. Also called
historical trauma; multigenerational
trauma; secondary traumatization.
("Intergenerational Trauma" 2022)

We have been talking about severe mental illness and
psychosis throughout this book, and I have written about
ways to heal yourself from generational trauma through
the trauma of caregiving for a person with severe mental
illness. Thus, this section is an expansion to highlight
reasons why you should do it.

Do we want to keep the avalanches falling slowly under
our care and the system of mental health the way it is now?
Do we want the apples to continue to feel like they can't
get away from the tree? Do we want to keep repeating
patterns of anxiety, depression, suicide, trauma, and abuse
in our families? Or do we want to change all that?

Generational Study

Research with mice has shown that fear can be passed
down through generations. Epigeneticists call this
transgenerational epigenetic inheritance. A study at
Emory University found that mice inherit specific smell

memories from their fathers, even when the offspring have never experienced that smell before and even when they have never met their father. The children were born with the same specific memory. With this method, researchers made mice afraid of a fruity odor, called acetophenone, by pairing it with a mild shock to the foot (Hughes 2013).

This indicated that trauma responses can be inherited through genetics, a fascinating finding. The scientists of the study talked about what this means for the future:

> "We have no idea yet," says Ressler, a practicing psychiatrist who has long been interested in the effects of post-traumatic stress disorder (PTSD). "But we think this would have tremendous implications for the treatment of adults [with PTSD] before they have children." (Hughes 2013)

When it comes to epigenetics, I cannot add more than the study above, as I am a therapist and not an epigeneticist. However, it is interesting to know there is scientific research that has found that stress responses can be passed down in generations through genetics alone, and not just learned social conditioning. These ideas are shifting the way we view trauma and mental health. Genetically speaking, the DSM-5 outlines all of the statistics related to mental health, including prevalence of each disorder within families. Thus, we already know so much about how mental illness can be passed on to family members. This study was just another validating reason we should be mindful of how trauma can be passed in family lines.

Considering this study, are you likely to change something that you currently do in response to stress or another behavior moving forward, knowing that your children could have that same response or reaction?

Generational Differences Currently

We are living in a very special time in history. In the year 2021, we had six different generations with six very different approaches to life. In this unique time, our grandparents, "the Traditionalists," are using technology but adhering to their old "work hard and don't complain" beliefs –the "you just do what you need to do" attitude. Their generation did not grow up with any technology, but we also have Generation Alpha, whose members are growing up only with technology, so they will never know the world any differently.

Consider this breakdown for reference.

1. Traditional Generation: born between 1900 and 1945. Currently over the age of 76.
2. Baby Boomers: born between 1946 and 1964. They are currently ages 57–75.
3. Generation X: born between 1965 and 1979/80. They are currently ages 41–56.
4. Millennials or Generation Y: born between 1980 and 1994/6. They are currently ages 25–40.
5. Generation Z: born between 1997 and 2012. They are currently ages 9–24.

6. Generation Alpha: born between 2012 and 2025. They are currently ages 0–9. ("Boomers, Gen X, Gen Y, Gen Z and Gen A Explained" 2021)

When it comes to mental health and personal growth and development, there has been a major shift across generations. Traditionalists don't typically attend therapy. Some may, but their generation didn't focus on mental health. They focused on working and providing stability. They didn't think of their emotions or have the same relationship with them as the younger generations now. Our baby boomer generation was so focused on work that there was an imbalance in self-care and between work and home life. Generation X shifted this. Since their parents didn't balance work and life, Gen X prefers to have the work-life balance. Millennials took that a step further; in addition to the work-life balance, they want self-development and to take care of their mental health. Millennials do things like take extra time off work and value self-care. Generation Z's views on mental health are the strongest. They believe in the value of therapy.

> In a report released by the American Psychiatric Association entitled "Stress in America: Generation Z" in October 2019, Gen Z were more likely to have received treatment or gone to therapy (37%) compared to Millennials (35%), Gen X'ers (26%), Baby Boomers (22%), and the Silent Generation (or Traditionalists) (15%).

Furthermore, Gen Z were more likely to report their mental health as fair or poor (27%), compared to their older counterpart generations, namely Millennials (15%) and Gen X (13%).

The reason for this trend of increasing use of mental health services and reporting mental health being poor is likely threefold:

- Life has introduced a different variety of stressors, leading to increased psychological concerns and more need for services for mental health.
- Awareness of mental health issues has grown, so that what once might have been ignored is recognized as a problem and treated as such.
- Stigma around using mental health services has lessened, making it more likely that Gen Z will identify their own issues and seek help when they feel they have a mental health problem that can be treated. (Cuncic 2021)

Thus, in summary, we are living in a time when newer generations have shifted the prevailing beliefs and values around mental health and why it matters. There is less stigma now than in previous generations and thus more opportunities for therapy. There are more opportunities for advocacy and discussion of mental health across all generations as well.

The point is that, when it comes to wanting to end generational trauma, we have data that supports the desire to do this across Gen Z, specifically, and many others. I am a millennial. (Don't kill the writer if you are a baby boomer or older.) I know from my experiences that millennials can talk to everyone in our lives about mental health as part of everyday conversation. And this isn't just because I'm a therapist; my nontherapist friends do the same. My millennial clients who aren't therapists are big on self-development, including life coaches, yoga, health and wellness coaches, and all disciplines that lead to well-rounded balance.

Thus, we have this amazing moment in evolutionary time when the generations who do believe in and value mental health could bust the system if we wanted to! We are already on our way there. We have the ability to shape the future to be more balanced physically, mentally, spiritually, environmentally, and all ways that lead to healthy and more natural living. We all want the same things; our missions are just different at times.

Social media, for example, gives us access to one another like we have never had before. This yields both positive and negative consequences. Yet some of the magic in having more access to one another is that we can see other healers around the country and world. I love going on TikTok and other platforms to see spiritual people and mental health practitioners talk about this very topic—healing generational trauma. We currently spend a lot of time thinking about our trauma and postulating ways to heal it so it doesn't proceed into future generations.

So many healers out there are practicing so many different methodologies, from Reiki to tarot or angel readings and physical health and wellness coaches. I can spend hours per week on TikTok alone watching these amazing souls talk about their specialties. We are all deeply craving for changes in our society. What a wonderful time to be alive! I truly cannot wait to see what the next decade brings in regard to mental health.

What matters is how we harness that awareness, advocacy, and planning for our mental health as a collective. Society can take paths that aren't healthy or paths on which we can choose to work together as a collective. And as we all know, different belief systems, aggression, politics, and religion are currently dividing us like never before. We have technology to further that narrative. We have technology to diminish that narrative also. It's a choice in how we all use that technology that matters.

It's so amazing to see that, for the first time in history, we have multiple generations believing in the value of work-life balance, mental health, and social justice. But again, how do we regulate through all of this and come out okay? It will take compassion, nonjudgment, and functioning from our heart chakras. It will take working together. We are; I am not implying that we are not. I am saying that shifts still need to happen to make this dream a reality.

We need to function from a place of love and light and not darkness, balancing the energies within all of us.

Just picture the year 2032, a decade away. Imagine us living in post–COVID times, all having learned so much from the experience of the pandemic and what we want the rest of our lives to look like. Imagine us feeling more healed than ever before, not just in a political context but living in a space of more compassion and peace because we worked hard to break generational trauma and indifferences as a collective.

How to Talk to Teens about Mental Health

In the school system, there has been a movement over the past couple of years to add mental health education to their curricula. There is legislation intended to elevate mental health education in schools. The focus is on teaching children about mental health and the multiple dimensions between physical and mental health, as well as how to get help and reduce stigma. This is great. Yet it is taking too long to get moving.

In the interim, we all know that teens talk to one another about mental health. I referenced earlier parents who catch these conversations happening among their teens and their friends, and many people have studied this.

So I want to give some tips for parents and families to refer to when they come across this issue. Before parents talk to their teens, they have to be self-regulated themselves. Parents need to provide authority, balance, and structure for their teens. However, they also need to provide love, belonging, and a safe space for them to feel validated, heard, and seen.

Thus, parents must go into this conversation removing their own judgments and expectations regarding mental health, and other topics that may come up in relation to it, that could be triggering for them. If they do not, their teens will feel unheard and shut down.

Proactive Steps to Talking with Your Teen

1. Autonomic Nervous System: Teach them about the autonomic nervous system and how it relates to our emotions and physical experiences. Teach them about self regulation skills—what they are and how to balance out the nervous system.

   Ask questions to facilitate dialogue with them:

   A. In what ways do you feel dysregulated at times?
   B. Where do you feel it on your body?
   C. What do you think in your mind?
   D. What are some of the ways your nervous system gets triggered—school tests, social interactions, and so on?
   E. What are some self-regulation skills you would be interested in trying—yoga, meditation,

breathing, muscle relaxation, visualization, other?

F. How can I support you more in times you feel dysregulated or in the overall managing of your feelings?

2. Normative Experiences in Adolescence: Teach teens what is normal to experience as a human in terms of anxiety, stress, sadness versus depression, generalized anxiety, and other diagnoses. Teach them about identity exploration in adolescents and that this is normal.

A. What is normal for adolescence includes the severity, intensity, and frequency with which you feel your feelings.

   i.   It is normal to feel stress, tiredness, hormone changes, general sadness, and some mood fluctuations; to want to feel and look good; to hope that our peers like us; and to have an occasional argument with a friend or some drama.

   ii. What crosses over to the mental health category is if you feel some of this more intensely or at higher rates. Maybe you feel a lot of this daily or hourly. You can't go to social outings because of your poor body image and worrying about what people will think of you. These things cause you a high level of distress.

   iii. We can talk to a professional about either side of the below chart at any time. The purpose is just to educate and validate that stress is normal and other aspects of adolescent development that are normal.

B. Ask your teen, "Based on this chart, what are your ratings? Can you share this with me? How can I help more?"

Typical in Adolescence	Off Balance/Need Help
Stress: Between 1 and 5 on a 1–10 **scale**	Stress or anxiety: 6–10 rating on a 1–10 scale
Identity questioning in any way (who I am, who I love, to whom I am attracted)	Questioning if I am LGBTQIA and just needing someone to talk to
Hormones fluctuating and changing moods	Moods change daily, hourly, and rapidly
General sadness: 1–5 on a 1–10 s**cale**	Depression, suicidal thoughts, more sadness, rating 6–10 on a 1–10 scale
Feeling tired/heavy need for sleep	Can't motivate myself for anything, or feeling unmotivated for more things than not motivated for.
Self-esteem, questioning if I am good enough	Questioning all the time if I am good enough— daily, hourly
Body image, questioning what I wear to school, if I look okay	Restricting food or change eating habits; feeling body image at a very intense level

Friend conflict	Constantly have friend conflicts, more often than not
Feeling a little anxious in social situations, between 1 and 5 on a 1–10 **scale**	Anxiety keeping me from doing things I love, or a consistently higher rating consistently of 6–10

3. Boundaries and Safety: Teach them about boundaries in sharing experiences and discuss where those boundaries are.
   A. What is safe and appropriate to share? With whom? How do we discern who is safe?
      i. It's okay to tell our closest friend a little about our situation.
      ii. It's safer to talk to parents, loved ones, or professionals.
      iii. Discern who is a true friend by determining who is most compassionate and understanding and doesn't gossip.
   B. What puts us at risk for bullying or other harmful situations?
      i. Putting personal things on the internet or social media
      ii. Anything in text or pictures carries a risk of being shared with others
      iii. Oversharing with people we only semitrust
   C. The How Tos: how to get help or ask for help for someone else who needs it.
      i. For yourself: talk to parent, school counselor, trusted friend, trusted loved one

    ii. For other friends: talk to school counselor, teacher, or other trusted adult in confidence about your concerns for your friend

4. Compassion: Teach them about compassion and empathy, religious/ethnic differences, and being heart centered.

    A. How can you tell when someone is compassionate and empathetic?

    B. Who are the people in your life you feel are empathetic?

    C. In what ways do you show empathy to others?

    D. In what ways is it hard to show empathy to peers?

5. Authenticity: Teach them about authenticity.

    A. Who are you underneath who you think you should be?

    B. What does *authentic* mean to you?

    C. How can you or we be authentic to who we are?

    D. What are your values and things that are important to you?

6. Encouragement/Collaboration: How can we get there together?

    A. How can we continue to talk and work together as family on this on an ongoing basis?

    B. What can we each do to ensure that we feel good continuing these talks?

    C. How can we do better as a family with each person's mental health and our stress levels as a family?

D. How can we encourage one another?

The cool thing about talking with teens is that, if you just provide the space for them to talk, they will unleash. I am not saying that parents need to be their children's therapists. I am saying that having an open, nonjudgmental stance with your child will be helpful. Setting boundaries with them is still what they need, including rules, expectations, and realistic consequences. Just remember not to give your child negative consequences if and when they open up to you. Thank them for being open and honest with everything they share.

Specifically, when it comes to the dynamic of a teen group having a group conversation about their mental health and they are all oversharing their symptoms and trying to relate to one another regarding mental health, a line needs to be drawn for them to understand the differences between the normative experiences discussed above. We need to teach them to not to be one another's therapists but their friends. Talk to them about the difference between those two roles.

Friends tend to listen for support; they don't try to change or overhelp the person. They validate their friends by saying things such as, "I am sorry you are going through this." They cross the line into trying to be therapists when they offer intervention advice they find on the internet or tell their friend what their own therapists told them. Being one another's therapists is not healthy. It exhausts all parties, and it's not helpful. It may be coming from a very compassionate place of offering advice, but it is a role we don't want our teens living.

10

Healing Together

In this book so far we have talked about how to get through the experience of caregiving for someone with a mental illness and how to focus on healing yourself through identifying with mental health. Now, we will focus on how to put it all together to heal as a family, as one. We will talk about ways to regulate our emotions together and ways family members, therapists, and support people can encourage regulation to the individual with psychosis or severe mental illness.

Coregulation in Families

Coregulation in families is defined as the supportive process between parents and children or young adults that fosters self-regulation development. It's an "interactive process of regulatory support that can occur within the context of caring relationships across the lifespan" (Rosanbalm and Murray 2017).

Typically, we think of coregulation in terms of the parent-child relationship. Parents have the most success helping with their children's regulation skills if they are fostering them within themselves also. If a parent is dysregulated and showing distress, a child may cry. If a parent is regulated and laughing, a child may laugh. There are three categories of support that parents typically use to foster coregulation. The first is providing a warm and responsive relationship, the second is structuring the environment, and the third is teaching and coaching self-regulation skills.

When I work with children with behavioral disorders and their parents, I talk to them about matching their affect to support the children in bringing their emotions down—in other words, to do the regulation skills with them. I typically follow general guidelines:

1. The parents develop a specific calm-down space in their home. They make the process of building the space interactive and fun. For example, they let the child pick fidget items and visuals they may want in their area.
2. The parents and child pick a consistent method of identifying feelings together as a family—for example, an emotions thermometer, an emotions color wheel, the four zones of self-regulation, or other method.
3. Together, parents and the child identify self-regulation tools that they relate with, such as

muscle relaxation, visualization, breathing exercises, yoga stretches, listening to something relaxing, or other tools.

4. The parents and child practice self-regulation when they are not escalated as part of their weekly routines. The parents will say to the child, "Mommy and Daddy feel X so we are going to practice muscle relaxation together." They praise the practice.

5. Then, when escalated moments arise, parents reinforce the use of the physical space and the regulation tools. If the child uses the calm-down space and some tools, parents positively reinforce that progress.

6. The important piece is that parents need to stay regulated during these interactions. They also have to model that it is okay to have these emotions. Children should never be punished for needing to use any of the above tools or the calm-down space.

Over time, the child learns several things: 1) It is okay and safe to have any emotion I experience, 2) It is okay and safe to talk about any feeling I have, 3) It is okay to take a break and do something soothing for myself, 4) It's normal for my parents to feel feelings too and need to use regulation skills, and 5) We can do all of this together.

The same holds true when I teach coregulation between adults. I even have a procedure I use with couples in marital counseling or any family therapy for people of any age, for that matter.

When I think of applying coregulation for people with severe mental illness and their loved ones, who are most likely adults—we may not have actual calm-down rooms and some things may be slightly different—I think of taking the ideas and principles in this book thus far and designing a coregulation form or curriculum for our population.

Psychosis and severe mental illness have their separate challenges. People with anhedonia, for example, do not know they are sick. So one precursor to any effective coregulation is working with the caregiver and loved one on accepting this. They cannot go into a coregulation session or attempt with any expectation that they will have an epiphany or aha moment when their voices and delusions will not be present or will somehow go away. However, we can hope or expect that we can reduce the intensity of the emotions and experience around the hallucinations or delusions and lessen their impact.

It's also important to remind and note that not every person who experiences psychosis has anhedonia. Some individuals can discern that their hallucinations or delusions are not real. It depends on the stage of their illness.

All we can ever manage is the experience and intensity of the emotions surrounding the psychosis symptoms. We can reduce the stress surrounding the need or want underneath the symptoms.

For example, most of my mother's hallucinations came as a result of an unmet need in her life surrounding safety, financial safety or security, the need for love and belonging, or physical health needs. When her voices would talk to her about money and settlements, her need was related to financial security. When her voices would chatter with me or family involved, she had a need for family time or love and belonging. When her voices would say they were coming to hurt her, she needed to feel safe, and when they would tell her to eat carrots from a can or that she was pregnant, she needed a physical health checkup. I am not implying that every delusion or hallucination has a need. I am saying that, if we directly ask people what their needs are instead of focusing on the voices, we can support them and get answers.

Thus, when working with an individual or family member with psychosis or severe mental illness, I can see that some steps would be useful in helping them work through and discern what the need is rather than the specific details of the psychosis (meaning settlements, etc.). Thus, in some ways, we are saying, "Let's work *with* the voices, not against them."

Regulation Steps

1. Grounding and self-regulation and safety in the moment: This would include telling the individual or loved one, "You are safe here where we are right now in this moment" and helping them look around the room to see seeing they are safe.

2. Meditations and intentions: This involves taking a moment to set intentions of the session of self-regulation: "We are here today to destress

together." Doing a startup meditation at the beginning helps relax the autonomic nervous system.

3. Identifying their want or need: Walk them through what their need is on a basic level.

4. Acceptance of the present voices as tools to what I need: Redirect the voices and accept them.

5. Planning to get my need met by X, Y, Z: Planning together to get the needs met.

6. Validation they are heard and safe: Tell the individual that their needs are heard and they are safe.

7. Reminder to trust intuition: If something doesn't feel good, we don't do it.

8. Heart coherence: Focus on aligning from the heart.

When talking to someone experiencing psychosis, here is an example of how to get to the base need:

> Tommy, I notice you are talking about money settlements today. Before we talk about that, let's take a minute to do this guided meditation together to ground ourselves and feel safe. Let's first regulate our bodies and minds. Are you noticing how your body physically feels? Where do you feel tense in your body? Do you feel racing thoughts? How intensely do you feel these things on a scale of 1 to 0? Let's do these grounding techniques together first.

Now that we are grounded and feeling lower on our stress scale, let's talk about the money settlements. I notice the theme is about money today. What do you need? Would money make you feel safe? What would make you feel safe? Can we tell the people you are speaking to that you are taking a break right now? I think that's what you are really feeling, right? Is your stress about money?

Can we use visualization for this need and create a picture in our minds of what the positive outcomes could be? How could we envision feeling safe and secure about money? What does that look like and feel like?

Now let's talk about how we can get there with some additional support.

Regulation Steps for the Caregivers

1. Safety: Work with the person to establish that they are safe. "I shouldn't fear my loved one's symptoms; they are just symptoms."
2. Meditations and intentions: State the intentions of the regulation session. Open with a meditation if the person wants to regulate their nervous system.
3. Identifying the want or need: Support the caregiver in identifying their need and what they

can do to get more of their needs met. Is it self-care time? A break? More natural supports?

4. Validation: Validate that they are heard and understood.

5. Balancing of heart chakra and heart coherence: What would make you feel aligned with your heart today and this week?

Coregulation for Loved One and Caregivers

After a little individual time with the person with severe mental illness and the caregivers, it's time to do a joint-coregulation session. This could be doing the above steps together, side by side. This could also be things such as a yoga session together, a joint Reiki session together, or other alternative holistic practice.

However, helping the family members match their energy, affect, and compassion is the goal. Complete coregulation sessions together weekly or as needed during the caregiving process. I wish I would have had the opportunity for this during my time with my mother. We do a lot of family therapy in the system now. However, it's traditional talk therapy, typically. And it misses the idea that regulation is needed in both parties to sustain any progress. If we regulate together in the session, we will regulate together outside of the session. If we cannot figure out a way to manage the big feelings or symptoms, we will continue to be unsuccessful.

So what I envision is this ongoing process of regulating together to create closeness and understanding of the process. The point of the coregulation session isn't necessarily for the caregiver or loved one to be able to express their feelings to the person with the mental illness. It is more about sitting in the fact that we can't always understand the other person or asking, "How can we be okay with the fact that we might not agree?" It's about understanding that our feelings may be different.

But again, all is safe and valid. Creating opportunities for this reduces the chance that the person with mental illness will not come back to treatment. They will be much more likely to return if given opportunities to feel safe, validated, and heard.

Joint Coregulation Steps

1. Again, create an environment of safety together.
2. Identify the rates and intensities each person is feeling—for example, "I feel my stress is an 8/10." Someone else may feel theirs is a 5/10. The focus isn't about what feelings are felt. It's about the underlying feeling or intensity that bonds the two. It's recognizing that we both have stress, so let's sit in it together.
3. Practice some self-regulation tools together: meditations, grounding, muscle relaxation, and so on.
4. Identify our needs as a family or team for this week and tell one another what they are.
5. Identify how we can all work from a heart-compassionate place this week or at this time.

In conclusion, I imagine that, had my mother and I had

this opportunity to regulate our nervous systems together through any part of the journey, it would have been a slight game changer. I don't think it will perfect things, yet it would make everyone feel validated, heard, regulated, and together on the same page. I truly believe that having these opportunities would have engaged my mother in therapy instead of causing her to feel "crazy" and associate therapy with that feeling.

11

Ideals for the Future

Throughout the last few chapters of part 3, we have explored generational trauma and ways to talk to teens about mental health in an effort to shape a different view of mental health. We also explored self-regulation steps for the individual, the family members, and how to do it jointly.

This chapter aims to take a brief look at different modalities of care and considerations for the future. It is my personal belief that changes in our mental health system would lead to many of the issues at hand being irrelevant in our future. This chapter explores a few key changes that could be made and an idealistic vision for the future.

I have referenced both conventional therapy techniques and spiritual techniques, loosely. There has been a shift in our culture that is leaning us toward more spiritual practices as part of therapy. Overall, spiritual psychology focuses on four attributes: physical (what you do), mental (what you believe), emotional (what you feel), and the authentic self (ability for joy, acceptance, and self-compassion; who you are to your core or soul level). ("What is Spiritual Psychology," 2020). Conventional psychology tends to leave out looking at things from your core soul level (Sol, 2022).

Some therapists believe in only a few modalities; others are eclectic. Some believe only in spiritual psychology. Yet this isn't a dissertation on psychology theory. This book is intended to highlight ways to get through the caregiving experience with some techniques and posit considerations for your own healing and generational healing.

The mind is just a tool. It is dualistic and assumes there are only two realities-good and bad, or negative and positive. At times, this causes us to get stuck in cycles. Consciousness, or spirit, is just who we are. Our physical bodies are vessels. All three components need support in any type of care.

Treating one without the others is irresponsible. How could we not treat the minds, bodies, and souls of individuals with severe mental illness? My mother's story and your story are evidence to this need. There are limitations to psychology as a stand-alone practice.

Mateo Sol writes:

> Psychology can become a poison and a cure at the same time. On one hand, it

points out all the ways in which we are "not good enough, emotionally stable enough, well-adjusted enough, healed enough" etc. etc. And on the other, it gives us all the tools to help us "get over" these pathologies (or give us the idea that we're getting over them—until we use psychology to condemn ourselves again). Furthermore, when spirituality lacks psychology it is disconnected, dissociated, insubstantial, and/or ungrounded. (2022)

Sol discusses in his article that both aspects are needed for true healing and uncovering all parts of ourselves, that we can't have one without the other as it creates an imbalance. I tend to agree with Sol, which is why I took a generally eclectic approach to discussing ways you can heal through apples and avalanches.

It's about using your own discernment in what you need, at the time you need it.

Group Therapy

My group-therapy hypothesis is that we have gone too far in separating mental health–specific diagnoses into their own group therapy sessions. We do this because it creates group cohesiveness, a feeling of being with people who experience the same situations (alcoholism or addictions, borderline personality groups, etc.). However, I believe that we have spent so much time separating the groups that we have lost the underlying idea that, no matter what you are going through in life, it is difficult.

The parent of a child with addictions and the child of a parent with a mental illness both experience the same underlying feelings: grief, loss, anticipation of symptoms, anger, and sadness. Thus, if we create some opportunities for mixed groups to get together, I believe that listening to stories that are different from ours, not all the same situationally, will bring about healing opportunities.

It would even further our ability to not feel alone, to feel and remember that everyone suffers from something, and to feel less isolated in specific groups. I am not saying that we should stop all disorder-specific groups, as they are very effective. I am asking to add as an option groups that focus on heart coherence in the experiences we all face. We are not alone in any pain we endure, as we all have pain. Learning about people outside of our experiences also heals.

Imagine a group with a parent of a child with addictions, a mother with a child with autism, a spouse of a person with bipolar with psychoses features, and ten others. Imagine what healing properties could come from listening to varying stories from one another. Imagine the compassionate healing properties!

It reinforces the idea that we are all one. We are not alone in our pain. We all suffer. We all heal.

My experience with my mother was a struggle. But I want to hear about the mother's fifteen-year struggle with her son who has low-functioning autism and how she has made it through that, how she does that every day. I want to hear about the granddaughter who is caretaking for her grandparent with dementia. I want to hear all these stories, as they help me realize I am not alone. This idea that people deal with different diagnoses in all these different ways is real. However, the underlying feelings are the same, and realizing that creates less isolation and more compassion.

When we put things in boxes, categories, or steps, whether it's diagnosing, treating, loving, grieving, or healing, we limit ourselves to a few possibilities. As humans, constructs like time exist to keep us organized and productive. Constructs like lists, steps, boxes, and classifications do the same for us—they keep us organized. Yet I feel they are so limiting. They are also time bound.

If we develop a theory, five years later we will have new thoughts and research on that theory. Then, we say, "Oh, we need to go back and modify that theory and change it." That's science for sure. Yet when it comes to mental health, categories, theories, and steps can hold us back in some ways. The one thing that always remains the same when it comes to a person's emotional well-being is that need for love and belonging.

The best soups are made when we don't follow exact recipes. Just a little bit of this, a little bit of that, gives the tastiest results. By this, I am not saying that changing all the ingredients would result in good soup. I am saying maybe we should consider this in this field of mental health care because it is not an exact science; it's okay to be eclectic in our approaches with our clients. We can use a little of this and a little of that depending on the clients' tastes. Open up doors and access to multiple disciplinary and holistic types of service lines to people with severe mental illness.

Types of Additional Healing Specialties

There are so many different healers in this world. I am only an infant in learning about different modalities. However, I could spend hours on social media watching the various formats. One day, I came across a person who uses a flute for music therapy healing. I have seen Reiki specialists making amazing videos and somatic-movement specialists doing videos on healing through dance. I have seen "light workers" using a combination of light codes and light language to help heal. There are so many inspiring, amazing, and unique healers out there using methods of embodiment psychology. You can feel the movement of Western and Eastern practices being gradually merged in our culture.

It brings a lot of hope to the world to realize that the opportunities for experiencing healing or living in compassion or your most authentic self are within reach in the burnt-out culture in which most of us are living.

Modalities of Care

Imagine walking into a multidisciplinary holistic office in the future. You, as the client or family, get to choose the services you need that week, and providers aren't scarce. You have a choice of therapist, spiritual coach, Reiki specialist, health and nutrition coach, primary care physician and nurse, expressive arts therapist, HeartMath specialist, somatic movement therapist, yoga therapist, case manager, massage therapist—you name it. Pick from the menu. It sounds idealistic, right? But some practices already have at two or three of these in one building. Imagine how much better care would be if we could target everything in one facility.

We currently aren't there as there are barriers to this. A few things would need to change first.

1. Insurance needs to change, including how billing is done for these services.
2. Laws around mental health and mental health services need to change.
3. Federal and state laws and systems need to change regarding funding for such programs.
4. Availability and scarcity of providers needs to be addressed. There are plenty of helpers and specialists, yet they are scattered.

For this type of care to exist, the whole system would need to crash and be rebuilt. We all know that insurance companies dictate who, what, when, where, why, and how we can receive treatment. The cost of one hour of therapy is typically $109. People will severe mental illness who are already living on medical assistance can only see providers who take that insurance. This is incredibly limiting since not all providers take all insurance types.

Big Pharma always wins. They don't want this change to happen, as they would lose their business. If people received holistic, well-rounded care, the need for medications would reduce. People would get better, get well. The social construct of the mental health system prevents people from wellness as it stands now. It limits possibilities.

The effects of changing a system like this would not only provide many more opportunities for the population of people suffering with any mental illness, but it would also reduce the likelihood of homelessness. It would reduce suicide rates. It would increase engagement in care itself, as who wouldn't wanted to be treated with options for care such as these. Incarceration rates would decrease. Heck, it would decrease overall aggression rates on this planet.

According to Statistica.com, the United States had a total of 12,472 mental health facilities in 2019 ("Number of Mental Health Treatment Facilities in the US in 2020 by Service Setting" 2020). This included hospital inpatient facilities, twenty-four-hour residential facilities, partial hospitalization facilities, and less-than-twenty-four-hour outpatient facilities. Earlier in the book, I mentioned NAMI's statistics of the number of people with mental illness in our country. NAMI also states that only 46.2 percent of adults with mental illness received treatment in 2020, just 64.5 percent of adults with serious mental illness received treatment, and 50.6 percent of youths aged six to seventeen received treatment. Do you see it? The numbers of people receiving treatment who actually need it are low.

NAMI further states that 134 million people live in a designated Mental Health Professional Shortage Area ("Mental Health by the Numbers" 2022). That's a big number. If doors opened to more variations of therapy modalities and holistic care, would access to providers and professionals increase?

I think you can tell I'd love to just break the system. However, I want to rejuvenate it, realign it, recenter it, refocus it, and redesign it. That is all. We all want that. It can be such a slow-moving change. In in the interim, for every year that slow change happens, roughly 50 percent of people with mental illness will not receive care for that year. Nothing changes if nothing changes. We need to move more quickly, before it's too late.

Imagine what could be different for you and your loved one if some of these barriers to treatment didn't exist. People with mental illness and severe mental illness deserve to be treated with respect, dignity, and compassion, just like every other human.

When You See Someone

(a child, spouse, parent, sibling,
grandparent, aunt, uncle)

When you see someone walking down the street, yelling
out loud to no one, let them be without judgment.
When you see someone sitting in a restaurant talking
to themselves, let them be without judgment.
When you see someone walking down
the street looking disheveled with bags of
groceries, let them be without judgment.
When you see a homeless person on the side of the
highway or in the city, let them be without judgment.
When someone tries talking to you about alien
and government conspiracies, have compassion.
When you see someone hyped up on drugs,
don't stop to take a video for social media.
Have integrity and compassion.
When you see someone dancing alone in the middle
of the street, let them be without judgment.
When someone tells you that the government
implanted a chip in their body, have compassion.
When you see anyone, of any age, having a meltdown
in public, let them be without judgment.

That person deserves compassion. You are looking at someone's loved one—someone's child, sibling, parent, grandparent, spouse, aunt, or uncle. Behind that person is a grieving family, missing them, longing to have them in their lives, longing for them to be healthy, and wondering if they are okay every day.

Before reacting or judging, use the Think model we learned as children. Think about what you want to say or do and ask yourself, *Is it true? Is it helpful? Is it inspiring? Is it necessary? It is kind?*

Also ask yourself, *Am I reacting to this person out of fear?* We all are afraid of the unknown or uncertain. And sometimes that fear makes us do humiliating things to others, such as recording a person with addictions for humorous or entertainment purposes and putting the video on social media without their consent.

That person who is struggling with addictions most likely got there after having trauma in their life. Have some integrity and compassion. Would you want someone recording you without your consent or recording your family member without consent?

Ask yourself, *Can I have compassion for someone else's reality? What about their reality makes me uncomfortable?* Our realities don't have to match in order for us to be kind. Imagine all the horrible things people have been through that led them to their current situations.

See the person for who they are. See their soul.

Talk to them as you would any other human. Just because someone has psychosis symptoms does not mean that they can't hear you or understand you. Their mind is just busier than yours.

Getting Back to the Soul

You can be Christian, Buddhist, spiritual, or atheist or believe in the Christ consciousness—it really doesn't matter. It's okay to have these different belief systems and still find the common route of compassion, understanding, and love.

Each soul's journey on Earth is uniquely different. Our passions and our purposes are all uniquely different. We incarnate on Earth with a soul contract, and for whatever reason we agree to our life paths before they are walked to enhance our souls' growth. (That's my belief, anyway.) So if you chose your soul contract to experience this life as an atheist, that's okay. Your soul wanted to experience that. What matters is that we aren't judging one another for those different belief systems.

I pose this question: If you believe in soul contracts and that people choose to experience the lives they have, including the lessons they learn, adversities they face, and family members they have, how does that change the way you perceive your life currently? How does that change the way you perceive mental health? What about how it changes the way you perceive your role as a caregiver?

And whether someone "awakens" during this lifetime is not for anyone to judge. A mass awakening is occurring in this year, at this time. The theory is that it's occurring to help raise the vibration of the planet in love during these chaotic times so that we can move to the "new Earth" of peace and unconditional love.

Wherever we are on our timelines, that is ours to experience. I accept myself at every stage of my timeline and development. I accept others at every stage of their timeline and development without judgment. Repeat that with me.

And faith is sovereign. You believe whatever you believe because it's your free choice to do so. We don't have to match on that to coexist. We just have to stay regulated in our differences. (I am pretty sure I wrote this already.)

Perfectionism is an illusion. We don't have to know everything, be everything, or do everything to be whole. Imperfection is itself perfection. Love is perfection. You are exactly where you are supposed to be at this very moment of your life, beautifully imperfect, living, and existing.

> I am a recovering perfectionist, and an
> aspiring good enough-ist. —Brené Brown

Everyone has an inner child. The businessman working day and night because, as a child, he grew up in scarcity and did not have his basic needs met has an inner child, as does the full-time working mom who is running her kids around like crazy to activities while also holding employment so her kids can have what she didn't as a child.

If we see people as their inner children in adult bodies, we can have more compassion for the behaviors they display as adults. And if we see ourselves in our adult bodies as our inner children, we can have more compassion for ourselves.

We are meant to be on this Earth to experience pain, which helps us love. Love helps us repair our pain as well as one another's pain. We are meant to connect and to coexist in the sharing of our hearts and souls in their purest forms.

I love my soul. I love your soul.

I have a beautiful soul. I say that humbly. I've spent thirty-nine years questioning everything about myself; from the freckles on my skin to the shape of my body to every interaction I have ever had with anyone. Pure neuroticism.

I invite you to say the same about your soul. Free yourself from self-judgments, limiting beliefs, and societal expectations. Be the authentic, amazing you.

Hi, I am Heather Scherf. I am a beautiful soul having a human experience, as are you. Because we are human, we cannot always be our most authentic selves. In my meditations I see myself as a woman of light and love wearing a rose-gold dress, with long hair and jewels on her head, and a white tiger as a pet, like something from a Disney movie.

In the real world I aspire to be like her, my soul, to be more congruent with her. But because we are humans, we must strip away all the conditions and societal pressures to be like our souls. And it's not about what she looks like but what she embodies and stands for—unity, peace, love, joy, calmness. Yet I will continue to make mistakes so that the soul can grow and evolve, and those are the magical and whimsical possibilities in our earthly experience.

Who are you? Who is your soul? What does your soul embody or represent?

And as a side note, why is it that, if something is whimsical, it is often perceived as neurotic? If I want to meditate and astral project on the weekends, roll around in mud, and then turn around during the week and ground myself to be able to work, what is that hurting? Let us howl at the moon if we so desire. If you see us, *mind yo business*.

Conclusion

When I started writing this book, my original intention was for it to be specifically for loved ones and caregivers of people with mental illness. I didn't realize just how much I'd be writing about healing generations to come. I wanted to speak to the population of people who, on average, spend thirty-two hours per week caregiving for the ones they love and the trauma associated with that. And my hope is that you have found some relatable points in this book, some tools, or some hope.

But as the writing went on during the year of 2022, with a worldwide pandemic, political unrest, and the potential start of World War III, this book ended with the importance of healing generational trauma. The world is cloaked in darkness right now, in pain. So while the original intent of the book was what it was, I think it naturally unfolded to healing ourselves individually and as a collective for our families and future generations.

I am not a political psychologist. I am not a spiritual counselor. I am a general licensed professional counselor in the state of Pennsylvania working in private practice, serving a variety of clients. But through my personal experience with a parent who had a mental illness and the medical disease of cancer, my work as a counselor, my own journey of healing my mental health around trauma, and seeing the world now, I can say that our political and worldly unrest is based in generational trauma. How could we not all agree on that by now?

We are all in pain. We all feel dysregulated during these times of unrest because of the political battles over the last several years and all that proceeded them. Anger, fear, and pride are the primary emotions we feel during these times, or when we watch the news. I am most certainly not the first person to say and think this, and I certainly won't be the last. And the emotions are contagious.

Living in fear, anger, and pride is a mental health-related issue. These are issues within our own souls. Everyone is upset about something due to their own experiences with that something. Whether it be political in nature, environmental, racial, or any of the current issues, we are acting on those because of our own experiences, relationships, and attachments to them.

They are everyone's reality. They are the results of generations of pain and hurt, no matter what side of any argument or debate you are on. All sides are hurting. I may not be the best therapist as every day and week I make mistakes. I could say something different to my clients at times, miss opportunities, or make other counselor mistakes.

But one thing I hold true as one of my strengths as a counselor is that I can always see both or multiple perspectives of the clients, couples, and families with whom I work. I can see all sides of their pain as individuals and members of their families. Everyone is justified in their pain. Everyone's feelings are right or valid. Agreeing with this statement and seeing it as true creates a better reality for us all to coexist peacefully in each of our realities.

The point is that, when we are leading with lower-vibrational emotions, war results. When we are leading with higher-vibrational emotions like compassion, grace, and love, war recedes and peace can exist. We could be talking about actual war occurring here in 2022, political wars, humanitarian wars, or metaphorical wars in our families or even within ourselves.

Yet the irony of it all is that, if we work on the wars within ourselves first, then the wars within our families and on the outskirts of all the -isms and larger-scale issues can be managed in a more calm, compassionate way. Thus, if we start with self-regulation and healing within ourselves as individuals, the rest of the world heals, shifts, and evolves, even if slowly.

I trust and have faith that it will come and can feel it coming. These transition years are taking us from what we know of life as it is now, with unrest, to this new place of peace, compassion, and living from a heart-centered place. This new world will have less stress, living to live, and not working to survive. It will be a place where we all transition into a new place of compassion, where there's less division but more unity and love. Can you see it?

The unfortunate part of that is that not everyone will go there. It's not like we can all just hit the magical reset button on our country or our planet. It takes active work from people to realize how they individually contribute to it and to want to change it. People have sovereignty in their choices. But imagine if 50 percent or 75 percent of the population made active choices to search within themselves to come from a more heart-centered space and then worked outwardly toward all other relationships in this world. It we look at our own souls, we heal and we then heal others because, inevitably, we are all one.

I even trust and have faith that this book will make its way to people who need to see it. I set the intention, "I'm not sure who needs to hear or read it, but I want it to make it to the hands of people who would benefit from it in some way." I hope caregivers of people with mental illness, family members, and people who have had their own struggles with mental health gained something from reading this. I hope you feel empowered to change your mindset around genetic precursors to mental illness and that you will not give so much power to them.

But getting back to the family members and caregivers of people who suffer from mental illness in some way, this is for you.

May You

May you have the hope you need, at the time you need it.
May you see that when you are healing that darkness
inside of you, whether it is through the caregiving
experience or other, that the balance of darkness
and light is possible again and will happen.
May you feel inspired to use some of these tools
within this book and explore them more on a
deeper level through your own journey.
May you feel permission to feel every single feeling you
feel without judgment of yourself, at the time you feel it.
May you feel permission to take breaks as
needed to get curious about yourself in any
way you need to, at the time you need it.
May you feel permission to look at your expectations
of yourself and modify or release them as needed.
May you feel permission to listen to your inner
child or your inner adolescent to heal and use
them as your guides to your own understanding
of yourself and your heart's desires.
May you refrain from judgment of yourself of any
kind in your mental health journey or any other
adversity you have experienced in your life.
May you have peaceful conversations among
friends in your journey with mental health.
May you feel your chakras open and use them
as needed in your journey, whether that is your
throat chakra wanting to speak your truth and
having the courage to do so or your heart chakra
to feel compassion for yourself and others.
May you feel your story—write it, journal it, tell
it, do something with it that feeds your soul.

I invite you now to do that. If you are interested, a survey is attached. A side intention of this book was to hear all your stories from the caregiving for people with mental illness. I want to know what you want. I want to take your direct feedback based on the responses you give and use them for something in the future. If I ever get the chance to work in a place of change, I want to have the information that comes from the souls who have lived, walked, and breathed mental health in their lives.

I may use the information you provide to write a follow-up article on my website or attempt to publish the responses somewhere. That is yet to be determined. The information you provide in the survey will be kept confidential in the sense that I will not release identifying information. I would only share your desires of what you would like to be different in the mental health system or in the types of care you receive.

May you have peace in your journey of this thing called life and enjoy playing on this big, beautiful, floating rock we call Earth. After all, we are all just here doing a round on Earth in our souls' journeys. Make it a good one.

Much love.

I carry your heart; I carry it in my heart.
Then I carry it to the next heart.

Appendices

Appendix A

Daily/Weekly Self-Care Check-In Tool

Date:_____

Current emotional energy level from chart: _____

How do I feel:

Physically_____

_____

Emotionally_____

_____

Mentally_____

_____

Spiritually_____

_____

Consult the following lists of tools based on the way you
are feeling. Choose the ones you feel would be useful today.
If you are feeling an imbalance physically, then it's time to
take a break and do something physical. If you are feeling
an imbalance emotionally or mentally, then it is time to
take a break to check in with yourself or release something.
If you are feeling an imbalance spiritually, it's time to talk
to someone you trust or engage in a spiritual check-in.

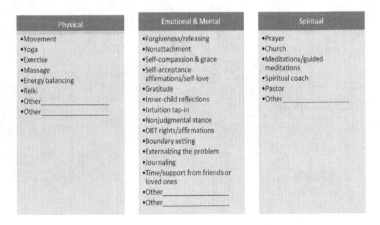

Physical	Emotional & Mental	Spiritual
•Movement	•Forgiveness/releasing	•Prayer
•Yoga	•Nonattachment	•Church
•Exercise	•Self-compassion & grace	•Meditations/guided
•Massage	•Self-acceptance	meditations
•Energy balancing	affirmations/self-love	•Spiritual coach
•Reiki	•Gratitude	•Pastor
•Other_____	•Inner-child reflections	•Other_____
•Other_____	•Intuition tap-in	
	•Nonjudgmental stance	
	•DBT rights/affirmations	
	•Boundary setting	
	•Externalizing the problem	
	•Journaling	
	•Time/support from friends or	
	loved ones	
	•Other_____	
	•Other_____	

Check in after you've done some of the above and rerate
your feelings and energy levels. What helped? Do you feel
more grounded? Do you feel less pressure? What shifted?

Physical_____

Emotional/Mental_____

Spiritual_____

Stay in tune with yourself over time by journaling this. See what works for you and keeps you balanced and regulated. Even if it was only a slight change, it is something.

Appendix B

Apples and Avalanches Ending Survey

The survey from below can be taken on the following website: https://sprw.io/stt-c02427 Or, by scanning the QR code with your phone. Your responses may be used in something published or blogged about later. Your confidentiality is important to me. No identifying information will be used in reporting your responses.

Part One: Demographic Information

1. Do you identify as a caregiver of someone with mental illness, as a person who is struggling with their own mental health, or both?
2. What is your age?
3. If you are the caregiver of a loved one, what is their age?
4. If you are a person who identifies with having mental health issues of your own, what, if any, diagnosis have you been given by professionals?
5. If you are a caregiver, what is their mental health diagnosis given by a professional?
6. If you are a caregiver of someone with mental illness, how many hours per week do you spend caretaking for your loved one at this time?
7. If you have a severe mental illness diagnosis, are you currently in some type of treatment? If so, what kind?
8. How much money do you spend per year on costs specifically related to mental health treatment (whether you are the caregiver or a patient)?
9. If you are a caregiver of a person with mental illness, how long have you been in this role?

Part Two: Your Experiences, Wants, and Needs

1. What positive experiences you have had in the treatment you have received?
2. What negative experiences you have had in the treatment you have received?

3. How would you rate your overall mental health treatment across your experiences?
4. If you answered the above question with "very satisfied" or "completely satisfied," what were the factors that contributed to this response?
5. I felt my treatment team was compassionate. (Likert scale)
6. I felt my treatment team was burnt out. (Likert scale)
7. If you or your family member(s) could have access to holistic and ancillary types of services and therapies not currently covered by insurance, which ones would you choose, if any?
8. What is the one thing you wish people understood about mental health?
9. What is one thing you would change specifically about the mental health system if you could?
10. Do you like the idea from the book about weekly or as-needed coregulation family sessions as part of mental health treatment centers?
11. Do you like the idea from the book about being able to walk into a mental health or holistic center and being able to choose what types of help you need that week?
12. Do you like the idea from the book about the "healing compassionately together group"? It deals with not having just specified-diagnoses groups but also having access to mixed diagnoses, situations, or healing group.
13. What else would you like to share about your story that is not addressed in the above questions?

References

"7 Stages of Grief—Going Through the Process and Getting Back to Life." Recover from Grief. March 2020. https://www.recover-from-grief.com/7-stages-of-grief.html

Ambiguous Loss. *About Ambiguous Loss*. 2022. https://www.ambiguousloss.com/about/

American Psychiatric Association. (2022) *Diagnostic and Statistical Manual of Mental Disorders (DSM-5)*. https://www.psychiatry.org/psychiatrists/practice/dsm

Axelrod, Seth. "Core Mindfulness Handout: Practicing Nonjudgmental Stance" (adapted from Marsha Linehan's *This One Moment: Skills for Everyday Mindfulness*). 2008. http://files.dbtskillspractice.webnode.com/200000107-0eb3e0fadb/Nonjudgmental%20Stance%20Handout%20and%20Worksheet.pdf.

"Boomers, Gen X, Gen Y, Gen Z and Gen A Explained." The Kasasa Exchange. July 6, 2021. https://www.kasasa.com/exchange/articles/generations/gen-x-gen-y-gen-z

Brown, Brené. *The Gifts of Imperfection*. Center City: Hazelden Publishing, 2010.

Browne, Sarah Jeanne. "4 Ways Trusting Your Intuition Is Your Superpower." October 2, 2021. https://www.forbes.

com/sites/womensmedia/2021/10/02/4-ways-trusting-your-intuition-is-a-superpower/?sh=4be1e5d5c8e6

Cherry, Kendra. "Unconditional Positive Regard in Psychology." Accessed on June 11, 2022. https://www.verywellmind.com/what-is-unconditional-positive-regard-2796005

Commonwealth of Pennsylvania Code 231 Rule 14.6. "Determination of Incapacity and Selection of Guardian." Retrieved from http://www.pacodeandbulletin.gov/Display/pacode?file=/secure/pacode/data/231/chapter8014/s14.6.html&d=reduce

Conrad, Marissa. "What Is Anticipatory Grief and How Does It Work?" Forbes Health. June 2021. https://www.forbes.com/health/mind/what-is-anticipatory-grief/

Cooke, Joseph R. *Free for the Taking: The Life Changing Power of Grace*. Ada: F. H. Revell Co., 1975.

Cuncic, Arlin. "Why Gen Z Is More Open to Talking about Their Mental Health." VeryWellMind. March 25, 2021. https://www.verywellmind.com/why-gen-z-is-more-open-to-talking-about-their-mental-health-5104730

Emmons, Robert. "Why Gratitude Is Good." Greater Good Magazine. November 16, 2010. https://greatergood.berkeley.edu/article/item/why_gratitude_is_good

Finch, Sam Dylan. "People-Pleaser? Here Are 5 Ways to Unlearn Your Fawn Response." Healthline.com. June 15, 2020. https://www.healthline.com/health/mental-health/unlearn-fawn-response

Frothingham, Mia Belle. "Fight, Flight, Freeze or Fawn: What This Response Means." Simply Psychology. October 6, 2021. https://www.simplypsychology.org/fight-flight-freeze-fawn.html

Hankins, Kristen Galli. (2022). "6 Steps for Tapping into Your Intuition and Trusting Yourself." The Daily Positive.

Accessed February 2022. https://www.thedailypositive.com/6-steps-for-tapping-into-your-intuition-trusting-yourself/

Hazeldine, Stuart, dir. *The Shack*. 2017. Summit Entertainment.

Hedtke, Lorraine. "Creating Stories of Hope: A Narrative Approach to Illness, Death, and Grief. *International Journal of Narrative Therapy and Community Work,* 35*(1, March 2014):4–19.

Hicks, Esther, and Jerry Hicks. "Emotional Guidance Scale." In *Ask and It Is Given*. Carlsbad, CA: Hay House Publishing, 2004. https://pepaeducation.com/wp-content/uploads/2021/07/Emotional-Guidance-Scale.pdf

Hughes, Virginia. "Mice Inherit Specific Memories, Because Epigenetics?" National Geographic. December 13, 2013. https://www.nationalgeographic.com/science/article/mice-inherit-specific-memories-because-epigenetics

Ingram, James. "Somewhere Out There" (song from *An American Tail*.) Originally released in 1986.

"Intergenerational Trauma." American Psychological Association. Accessed February 2022. https://dictionary.apa.org/intergenerational-trauma

"Interpersonal Effectiveness." Dialectical Behavioral Therapy. Accessed on June 12, 2022 https://dialecticalbehaviortherapy.com/interpersonal-effectiveness/

Jeffrey, Scott. "A Definitive Guide to Jungian Shadow Work: Get to Know and Integrate Your Dark Side." CE Sage. Accessed on June 12, 2022. https://scottjeffrey.com/shadow-work/

Lanese, Nicoletta, and Scott Dutfield. "Fight or Flight: The Sympathetic Nervous System." Live Science. February 9, 2022. https://www.livescience.com/65446-sympathetic-nervous-system.html

Lavoie, Sarah. "Walter Cannon: Stress and Fight or Flight Theories." Study.com. 2022. https://study.com/academy/lesson/walter-cannon-stress-fight-or-flight-theories.html

Luna, Aletheia. "6 Ways to Practice Non-Attachment (and Find Inner Peace)." LonerWolf. February 10, 2022. https://lonerwolf.com/non-attachment/

Magnetize Yourself. "Powerful 7 Chakra Meditation to Identify Chakra Blocks." Video. YouTube. January 2021. https://www.youtube.com/watch?v=xipc8OaR22c

"Mental Health." National Institute of Mental Health. January 2022. https://www.nimh.nih.gov/health/statistics/mental-illness

"Mental Health by the Numbers." National Alliance of Mental Illness. Last updated February 2022. https://www.nami.org/mhstats

"Narrative Therapy." Good Therapy. Updated June 18, 2018. https://www.goodtherapy.org/learn-about-therapy/types/narrative-therapy

Neff, Kristen. "Definition of Self Compassion." Self-Compassion. Accessed January 2022. https://self-compassion.org/the-three-elements-of-self-compassion-2/

"Number of Mental Health Treatment Facilities in the US in 2020 by Service Setting." Statistica.com. 2020. https://www.statista.com/statistics/450277/mental-health-facilities-in-the-us-by-service-type/

Paddision, Sara. The Hidden Powers of the Heart. Boulder Creek: HeartMath, 1998.

Regan, Sarah. "Everything to Know about Ego Death: From What It Is to How It Happens." Accessed February 2022. https://www.mindbodygreen.com/articles/ego-death

Roedel, John. "Become, Become, Become." Accessed January 2022. https://www.johnroedel.com/post/manage-your-blog-from-your-live-site

Rosanbalm, K. D., and D. W. Murray. "Caregiver Co-regulation across Development: A Practice Brief." OPRE Brief #2017-80. Washington, DC: Office of Planning, Research, and Evaluation, Administration for Children and Families, US. Department of Health and Human Services. October 2017. https://fpg.unc.edu/sites/fpg.unc.edu/files/resources/reports-and-policy-briefs/Co-RegulationFromBirthThroughYoungAdulthood.pdf

Salow, Sylvia. "Learn the Difference between Feminine and Masculine Energy." Medium. December 11, 2018. https://medium.com/thrive-global/learn-the-difference-between-masculine-and-feminine-energy-ff1c14366aed

"The Science of HeartMath." HeartMath. 2021. https://www.heartmath.com/science/

Sengwe, Stephanie. "Hey People Pleasers: You Need to Watch Out for Fawn Trauma Response." PureWow. July 23, 2021. https://www.purewow.com/wellness/what-is-fawn-trauma-response

Sol, Mateo. "Spiritual Psychology: Why Meditation Isn't Enough." LonerWolf. February 11, 2022. https://lonerwolf.com/spiritual-psychology/

Stelter, Gretchen. "A Beginner's Guide to the 7 Chakras and Their Meanings." Healthline. Updated on December 18, 2016. https://www.healthline.com/health/fitness-exercise/7-chakras

"Stress in America: A National Mental Health Crisis." American Psychological Association. October 2020. https://www.apa.org/news/press/releases/stress/2020/report-october

"Trauma." American Psychological Association. 2022. https://www.apa.org/topics/trauma

Warren, Rick. *The Purpose Driven Life*. Grand Rapids: Zondervan, 2002.

"What Is Spiritual Psychology?" The Clearing. 2020. https://www.theclearingnw.com/spiritual-psychology

"What Schizophrenia Is Not." Mental Help.Net. 2022. https://www.mentalhelp.net/schizophrenia/what-it-is-not/

White, Taneasha. "Defining—and Addressing—Toxic Masculinity." Healthline.com. May 21, 2021. https://www.healthline.com/health/toxic-masculinity

Wikipedia. s.v. "unconditional love." Accessed June 2022. https://en.wikipedia.org/wiki/Unconditional_love

Yogapedia. "What Does Metta Mean?" Accessed January 2022. https://www.yogapedia.com/definition/7603/metta

About the Author

Heather Scherf, MS, LPC, is a licensed professional counselor in Pennsylvania who works with people from age three through adulthood. She earned a master's degree in counseling psychology from Chatham University. She has worked in a variety of clinical settings, including outpatient and private practice offices, home/community-based programs, and research-based programs. She has training in behavioral therapy, grief, and loss concerns and is a certified HeartMath specialist.

Printed in the United States
by Baker & Taylor Publisher Services